The Banking Law Reference Guide for National Banks

Second Edition

The Banking Law Reference Guide for National Banks
Second Edition

Jonathan L. Levin
Partner

Cohen, Shapiro, Polisher, Shiekman and Cohen

New York Institute of Finance

New York London Toronto Sydney Tokyo Singapore

Library of Congress Cataloging-in-Publication Data

Levin, Jonathan L.
The banking law reference guide for national banks / Jonathan L. Levin. -- 2nd ed.
p. cm.
ISBN 0-13-093972-2 (soft)
1. National banks (united States)--Outlines, syllabi, etc.
2. Banking law--United States--Outlines, syllabi, etc. I. Title.
KF1000.L48 1991
346.73'0821223--dc20
[347.306821223] 90-28483
CIP

This publication is designed to provide accurate and authoritative information in regard to the subject matter covered. It is sold with the understanding that the publisher is not engaged in rendering legal, accounting, or other professional service. If legal advice or other expert assistance is required, the services of a competent professional person should be sought.

From a Declaration of Principles
Jointly Adopted by
a Committee of the American Bar Association
and a Committee of Publishers and Associations

Printed in the United States of America

10 9 8 7 6 5 4 3 2 1

PREFACE

The genesis of *The Banking Law Reference Guide for National Banks* came a decade ago during my tenure as a Senior Attorney with the Office of the Comptroller of the Currency. With bank regulation increasing rapidly in complexity, the need was apparent for an organized means of access to the disparate body of law governing the national banking system. My initial catalogue and summary, corresponding to the compilation of laws in *The Comptroller's Manual for National Banks*, was published by the OCC from 1983 to 1985 as *The Manual Users Guide.* The first edition of the *Reference Guide*, published in 1988, enlarged the scope of the original work, refined the overall format and added OCC Banking Circulars to the survey of the law.

The Banking Law Reference Guide for National Banks, Second Edition constitutes a further expansion in scope and a quantum improvement in the utility of the work. I have updated the catalogue to reflect the extensive changes engineered by the Financial Institutions Reform, Recovery and Enforcement Act (FIRREA), as well as a variety of other new laws, including several affecting securities activities and money laundering. Perhaps more significant, I have created a comprehensive index to all the national banking laws. The index will, for the first time, enable the user to explore individual banking issues,while the catalogue will continue to provide a structural logic to the broader subject areas.

As were the earlier versions, the *Reference Guide, Second Edition,* will be a particularly useful resource for bankers, bank examiners, legal counsel, accountants, and students of banking law. Because FIRREA now extends the reach of national banking law to many areas of thrift activity, this volume also will have special relevance for thrift industry officials, thrift examiners, and thrift counsel.

A work of this scope reflects more than the efforts of a single author. I was most fortunate to have had the able assistance of several individuals to whom I owe my sincere appreciation. Much of the credit for the successful construction of the index rightfully belongs to Jessica Goldman, who also served as my dedicated taskmaster and editor in seeing the project through the summer. Linda Jacobs, my chief apprentice for the first edition, also deserves thanks for her editorial and drafting contributions in the later stages of production. Thanks go, as well, to Ann Marie Gorman and Nancy Stanton for their painstaking proofreading of the final text and to Anita Campbell-Lee for her insightful critique of the historical perspective. No less than with the first edition, I am deeply indebted to my secretary, A. Nayan Hamill, without whose artistic talent and technical proficiency the *Reference Guide* would not have reached completion. Just as essential to the success of this work were Susan Barry, acquisitions editor and Sheck Cho, managing editor at NYIF and Joan Kalkut, copy editor, all of whom have my lasting appreciation for their professional and personal dedication. Finally, I am especially grateful for the encouragement and patience of my wife Sharon, my daughter Natanya, my son Jared, and my partners at Cohen, Shapiro, Polisher, Shiekman and Cohen.

Jonathan L. Levin
Philadelphia, Pennsylvania
December, 1990

HOW TO USE THIS REFERENCE GUIDE

The Banking Law Reference Guide for National Banks, Second Edition is a unique tool designed to provide the user with ready access to the broad framework of federal laws governing the operation of national banks. The scope of the volume corresponds generally to the compilation of laws in *The Comptroller's Manual for National Banks,* published by the Office of the Comptroller of the Currency (OCC), the federal agency responsible for supervising the national banking system.

The *Reference Guide* is organized as a catalogue, separating all provisions of national banking law into fifteen chapters, each chapter embracing a major sphere of banking activity. Within each chapter, statutes are listed first, followed by regulations, OCC Interpretive Rulings and OCC Banking Circulars. Entries are ordered sequentially according to their respective citation to the United States Code (USC), the Code of Federal Regulations (CFR), or assigned Banking Circular (BC) numbers. OCC Interpretive Rulings are codified as Part 7 of Title 12 of the CFR. OCC Banking Circulars are permanent issuances, often carrying the force and effect of law, that relate to topics of supervisory concern to the OCC.

The *Reference Guide* also provides a shorthand summary of each provision within a chapter. The title of each provision, listed in the left margin, is the one officially assigned by the codifiers of the USC or the CFR, or by the OCC, as appropriate. Most titles are descriptive and are intended to be read in conjunction with the text in the right margin for continuity of substance. The word *bank* denotes *national bank* unless otherwise modified.

Located at the end of the *Reference Guide* is a comprehensive index keyed to particular national banking issues and pursuits. The index is both a page reference table and a citator to sections of pertinent law. For any single entry, statutes are cited first (sequentially by their numerical codification in the USC) followed by regulations and OCC Interpretive Rulings (sequentially by their numerical codification in the CFR) and then OCC Banking Circulars (sequentially by their assigned "BC" numbers). Crossreferences to related index entries are also provided, where appropriate, in bracketed format.

The survey of the law is current as of December 1, 1990, and necessarily will fall out of date as laws are revised, added, or removed. Accordingly, users are encouraged to consult relevant source documents for verification of the content of particular provisions.

The Banking Law Reference Guide for National Banks, Second Edition, *is not intended to constitute independent authority in support of any legal analysis or official action. If legal advice or other expert assistance is required, the user should engage the services of a competent professional.*

LIST OF ABBREVIATIONS

Agencies

EEOC	Equal Employment Opportunity Commission
FCA	Farm Credit Administration
FDIC	Federal Deposit Insurance Corporation
FFIEC	Federal Financial Institutions Examination Council
FHA	Federal Housing Administration
FHLMC	Federal Home Loan Mortgage Corporation
FRB	Board of Governors of the Federal Reserve System
FRS	Federal Reserve System
FTC	Federal Trade Commission
GAO	General Accounting Office
GNMA	Government National Mortgage Association
HUD	U.S. Department of Housing and Urban Development
MSRB	Municipal Securities Rulemaking Board
NASD	National Association of Securities Dealers
NCUA	National Credit Union Administration
OCC	Office of the Comptroller of the Currency
OTS	Office of Thrift Supervision
RTC	Resolution Trust Corporation
SBA	Small Business Administration
SEC	Securities and Exchange Commission
USPS	U.S. Postal Service
VA	Veterans Administration

Laws

BC	Banking Circulars (permanent OCC policies and standards)
CFR	Code of Federal Regulations (Federal regulations and interpretive rulings)
USC	United States Code (Federal statutes)

Other

GAAP	generally accepted accounting principles

CONTENTS

U.S. BANKING LAW IN HISTORICAL PERSPECTIVE

Banking. A simple word. Yet it conjures up a world of ideas: from dropping coins into porcelain pigs to depositing payroll credits into transaction accounts; from cashing personal checks to arbitraging Eurodollars; from funding home loans to financing corporate buyouts. How far we have come from that day when an early Venetian moneychanger first brought his "banco" to the town square!

Banking as we know it really did not begin in earnest until well after the birth of our nation. The early history of the United States witnessed the development of a fragmented and exceedingly localized banking industry. It seemed that virtually every town and hamlet boasted a bank, chartered by its state, that served as the center of its economic life. In those days a bank would regularly issue its own notes, which circulated as currency in the local vicinity. The arrangement worked well as long as people stayed close to home, but those bitten by wanderlust soon discovered that hard currency, *specie,* was the only universal medium of exchange between communities. Thus, attempts were made to institute a national monetary exchange, notably the two ill-starred Banks of the United States, but the young nation, fearful of the corruptive potential of concentrated financial power, needed a convincing reason to establish an effective, permanent system. That reason came with the onset of the Civil War.

As the battles flared and the war intensified, the demand for new recruits grew more urgent. President Lincoln soon faced a critical shortage of manpower, attributable in no small part to the absence of an acceptable mechanism for the payment of Union troops. State bank notes were useless over the wide reach of the battleground. A national currency in the form of notes backed by the Federal Government was the only answer, and Congress responded with the National Currency Act of 1863. A year later that law was transformed into the National Bank Act of 1864, a blueprint for financial strength and safety.

With the advent of a national currency and a network of federally chartered "national banks" to circulate it, the original intent was to tax state bank notes so heavily that state-chartered banks would fade quickly from the national landscape for lack of profitability. However, little did the grand planners envisage the ingenuity and resiliency of the state banking system. Note circulation did become unprofitable, but deposit and lending activities took on new prominence. The financial needs of the local populace did not abate, and the newly founded national banks could not satisfy the demand alone. Thus, by historical accident and economic necessity, the peculiarly American "dual banking system" was born.

As twin types of banks emerged, twin lines of regulation also evolved, each rooted in the premise that banking is a solemn public trust. The Office of the Comptroller of the Currency (OCC), created by the National Bank Act to charter and supervise national banks, began to develop policies and train examiners, while the states strengthened their own banking departments to monitor the business of state banks.

By the turn of the Twentieth Century, banking was fast becoming the most heavily regulated U.S. industry. The Panic of 1907, only the latest of the cyclical upheavals in which many banks failed, generated a fundamental change in American thinking. Out of the financial ruin emerged a consensus that a central bank was essential to the economic stability of the nation. Congress deliberated long on the plans, and in 1913 the Federal Reserve Act brought forth the Federal Reserve System, charged with crafting monetary policy and managing the payments system.

Two decades later, when the nation plunged into the Great Depression, Congress moved decisively to restore confidence in the banking system by enacting two monumental pieces of legislation, the Banking Act of 1933 (popularly known as the Glass-Steagall Act) and the Home Owners' Loan Act of 1933. Through the former, commercial banking was divorced from investment banking and the first bank deposit insurance program was instituted. Through the latter, the thrift industry was reconstituted for the express purpose of promoting home ownership, and a thrift deposit insurance program was launched. With new federally chartered savings and loan associations joining state-chartered thrifts, a dual system of thrifts emerged alongside the dual banking system. Thus, not only did federal-state duality persist and replicate, but the nation now also accorded formal recognition to the bank-thrift dichotomy.

Although few sessions of Congress adjourned without considering banking legislation in the years closely preceding and following 1933, little else of critical import to the structure and operations of the banking industry was produced. Granted, in 1927 the McFadden Act had awarded branching rights to national banks, in 1935 another Banking Act fine-tuned many of the 1933 provisions, and in 1950 the Federal Deposit Insurance Act reorganized the FDIC. However, not until 1956 did a fresh approach to banking begin to take hold.

The Bank Holding Company Act of 1956, and its substantial amendment in 1960, laid the groundwork for the controlled expansion of banking far beyond traditional limits by authorizing affiliation of banks with an ever-widening range of "closely related" businesses. Examination and enforcement powers with federal bank regulators were strengthened substantially with the enactment of the Bank Supervisory Act of 1966, and the general banking public became a special Congressional protectorate under the Consumer Credit Protection Act of 1968 (popularly known as the Truth-in-Lending Act).

Except for a raft of consumer protection statutes, banking law lay fairly dormant through most of the next decade. Then, in 1978, enactment of the Financial Institutions Regulatory and Interest Rate Control Act spearheaded a new campaign to recast the framework of bank regulation and, ultimately, the structure of the banking industry on a grand scale. Through that piece of legislation, federal bank regulators received far more extensive authority to interpret and enforce the legal matters committed to their jurisdiction. Also, it created the Federal Financial Institutions Examination Council, the first attempt to coordinate the standards and procedures followed by the widely disparate federal regulatory apparatus.

The watershed arrived in 1980. Throughout the 1970s bankers joined in a crescendo of criticism against the authority of thrift institutions to pay slightly higher interest rates on savings, thereby giving them a competitive advantage in attracting deposits. The cry for a "level playing field" was answered conclusively with the enactment of the Depository Institutions Deregulation and Interest Rate Control Act of 1980. That law accomplished two coordinate purposes: it fixed a schedule for phase-out and elimination of the interest-rate differential by 1986, and it granted broader powers to thrift institutions as a recompense for the loss of competitive advantage.

Proceeding inexorably towards interest-rate parity, both the banking and thrift industries grew increasingly concerned about their relative competitive positions. Only two years after enactment of the 1980 Act, the groundswell of anxiety prompted passage of yet another major piece of legislation, the Garn-St Germain Depository Institutions Act of 1982. That law conferred a "Christmas tree" of new powers on all types of financial institutions, from raising the national bank lending limit and unshackling national bank real estate loans, to easing usury ceilings on loans made by all federally insured depository institutions, to authorizing, for the first time, federal thrifts to make commercial and consumer loans.

An advance in the legislated deadline for interest-rate parity put banks and thrifts on an equal footing by the beginning of 1985. Competition between banks and thrifts grew heated as the two industries vied head-to-head for business. The distinction between the various types of financial institutions was lost on all but the most sophisticated customers. Not only was a commercial bank a "bank," but savings banks, savings and loan associations, and even credit unions had become "banks" to the average consumer of financial services.

Unfortunately, in the final analysis, thrift institutions were not banks. Indeed, most thrifts were, consistent with their original purpose, simple community-oriented businesses dedicated to the American dream of home ownership. Thrust into the turbulent waters of high finance and forced to compete for profits against sophisticated regional and multi-national banking giants, those institutions became easy prey for fast-buck promoters, high-living executives, and agents of organized crime.

The current thrift crisis materialized out of a fog of well-intentioned regulatory initiatives. Few in government or industry were so prescient as to recognize the pernicious temptations that were to be the fruit of a beneficent equalization of bank and thrift powers. By 1987 the situation demanded attention. The FSLIC was experiencing a rapid depletion of funds from a growing number of bankrupt thrifts, and the FDIC was pressing for expanded powers to salvage faltering banks. After considerable debate and compromise, Congress produced the weighty Competitive Equality Banking Act of 1987 (CEBA), which reached out like an octopus to close widening loopholes in the bank regulatory framework, recapitalize the FSLIC, streamline and reinforce federal thrift regulation, facilitate interstate bank acquisitions, reduce the time allowed for banks to withhold funds deposited by check, and place interest-rate caps on newly popular adjustable-rate mortgage loans.

It did not take long to discover that CEBA was weak and overextended. Deterioration of thrift institutions continued at a quickening pace. In a rush near to panic, Congress confronted the unfolding nightmare immediately upon reconvening in 1989. The result of their labors was the Financial Institutions Reform, Recovery and Enforcement Act of 1989 (FIRREA), a massive restructuring of the thrift industry and the overall regulatory environment.

FIRREA took a multi-tiered approach to resolving the debacle. First, it abolished the original, independent thrift agencies -- the Federal Home Loan Bank Board and the FSLIC -- and transfered their regulatory authority to a new Office of Thrift Supervision (OTS) within the U.S. Treasury Department. Second, it transfered all thrift deposit insurance functions to the FDIC, by establishing two separate insurance funds, the Bank Insurance Fund (BIF) for bank deposits and the Savings Association Insurance Fund (SAIF) for thrift deposits. Third, it created the Resolution Trust Corporation (RTC) to oversee the management and liquidation of thrifts that are declared insolvent by the OTS.

On a parallel front, FIRREA dug into the heart of thrift operations and powers. It severely restricted the lending authority of all thrifts, but especially hamstrung the loan activity of capital-deficient institutions. It established rigorous new minimum capital requirements for thrifts and imposed generally accepted accounting principles (GAAP) on an industry that historically maintained its financial statements according to the more flexible regulatory accounting principles (RAP). Attacking an area of considerable abuse, FIRREA also removed all direct equity investment authority from thrifts. Finally, in an attempt to return thrifts to a more prudent course, FIRREA embraced national banking standards as the principal regulatory frame of reference.

Although FIRREA is firmly implanted as of this writing, thrift fortunes have continued to deteriorate, and a sense of impending calamity has begun to weigh heavily on the banking system, as well. Fearing the worst and wanting to bolster government efforts to identify and punish those responsible for the current crisis, Congress closed its latest session with the enactment of the Crime Control Act of 1990. Title XXV of this omnibus crime bill launches the Comprehensive Thrift and Bank Fraud Prosecution and Taxpayer Recovery Act, which limits benefits to institution-affiliated parties, enhances governmental power to confiscate illicit assets, and expands the range of regulatory enforcement actions disclosable to the public. Of greatest significance in Title XXV, however, is Subtitle H, the Financial Institutions Anti-Fraud Enforcement Act of 1990. This new law, which offers substantial incentives for private citizens to join with Federal authorities in bringing wrongdoers to justice, is destined to flood the nation's courts with criminal prosecutions and asset recovery actions for decades to come.

Such is the historical context of American banking law, but what of the future? Two prominent trends augur a sweeping metamorphosis.

Consider the first trend: homogenization. Both in perception and in practice financial institutions of every stripe have become nearly indistinguishable. On a basic functional level, virtually every institution, be it bank or thrift, offers checking and savings accounts, consumer and commercial loans, and assorted auxiliary services, such as credit cards, safety deposit facilities, and financial counseling. Certainly, important distinctions do still exist, but they are esoteric and increasingly less relevant to the general banking public.

FIRREA, more than any other single factor, has sealed the fate of the thrift industry. It is difficult to imagine the long-term survival of the thrift institution as a distinct financial intermediary in the wake of a law that has decimated the lending limit, redoubled the capital requirement, and extinguished all but the most conservative means of investment. As if the death knell were not manifest enough, a clarion signal has been sounded by the reorganization of thrift regulatory authority under the Treasury Department umbrella. There, side-by-side with the OCC and constantly obligated to measure its own standards against the national bank benchmark, the OTS seems certain to succumb first to cross-fertilization, then assimilation and, ultimately, dissolution.

As the transition takes hold, what are its implications for the dual banking system? Within the realm of commercial banks it still sets the norm, but it, too, has lost a measure of its inviolability. The Federal Reserve continues its seemingly relentless pursuit of control over state bank subsidiaries of bank holding companies through its pervasive Bank Holding Company Act powers. Couple that with the FDIC drive to protect the deposit insurance fund by attempting to impose a variety of constraints on the activities of insured state banks, often in contradistinction to state law, and the line between federal and state banking identity begins to blur. A similar fate awaits the dual thrift system, as the OTS and the FDIC move to consolidate their respective powers over both state and federal thrifts.

So, thrifts are dying, and state banks are fast detaching from their state roots. The likely outcome, perhaps by the turn of the century, is a Darwinian evolution of the strongest thrifts into banks by means of bank holding company acquisitions and legislatively facilitated charter conversions. State banks, in contrast, are likely to remain linked to their respective state identities, but the meaning of the distinction seems destined to fade as state banking authorities are forced to defer increasingly to the paramount interests of the federal safety net. The only certain survivors of these changing times will be the national banks, a result ironically similar to that intended by the original framers of the national banking system.

Consider now the second trend: specialization. This trend has invaded the banking scene like a natural force, seeking to fill the vacuum created by homogenization. As likely as it may be that all financial institutions will eventually share the same nominal identity, it is just as certain that the financial needs and demands of the American people will only proliferate in their variety. Driven by competitive forces, banks can increasingly be expected to focus on tailoring their products and services to the requirements of specific economic sectors.

This concept of "niche banking" is not really new. The thrift industry is a prime example of targeting a limited financial sphere, namely, the housing market. Nonetheless, amid the complexities of contemporary banking, only the most diversified and sophisticated institutions can expect to provide the full range of commercial and consumer services. Consequently, out of practical necessity, almost every bank will be engaged in an active search for a suitable customer base and market niche. As fortune would have it, the same complexities have mobilized the banking public to mount a search of their own for institutions that can relieve the confusion by specializing in particular types of services.

Signs of an emerging new stratification in banking are manifest. Although nomenclature may change, needs do not, and already institutions are moving into the breach at every stratum. Small, community banks are regularly usurping the traditional role of thrift institutions with their unmistakable orientation towards the consumer. In urban districts across the nation new banks have sprung up for the express purpose of serving a professional and entrepreneurial clientele that has felt neglected by more sizable institutions. Having grown markedly in size and sophistication in recent years, larger regional banks have committed their resources to supporting the general flow of commerce within their market areas. At the upper end sit the multinational money-center banks. These financial megaliths often profess, as do the regionals, to consider the needs of all economic sectors, but their mission, in fact, centers principally on servicing major interstate and international enterprise.

Change on the operational side invariably is met by change on the regulatory side. Specialization is no exception. For years, powerful voices within the Federal government have been advocating restructuring of regulatory authority along functional lines. The Securities and Exchange Commission (SEC) is pressing with increasing vigor to inherit supervision of bank securities activities from the federal banking agencies. At various times in recent memory the OCC and the Federal Reserve Board have called for a realignment of jurisdiction over bank holding companies. The Bush Administration is also primed to play a more active role. Now that the Treasury Department houses both the OCC and the OTS, linkage of those two agencies to facilitate common regulation of functionally similar institutions is a genuine prospect.

Admittedly, predictions are only as good as the credibility of the signposts that inspire them. Nonetheless, for banking, one fact seems incontrovertible: No modern nation can survive, let alone prosper, without a banking system that anticipates the needs of the citizenry and advances to meet the challenge. Banks ultimately provide the medium for economic and social growth by managing the accumulation and transfer of wealth. We are living in turbulent times, turbulent in the nature of events and turbulent in the pace of change. Both the banking industry and the bank regulatory process have no alternative but to respond with heightened sensitivity and resolve to the new directions unfolding before us.

1

INTERNAL OCC ORGANIZATION

STATUTES

12 USC

1 *Comptroller of the Currency:*	establishes bureau • Comptroller heads under general directions of Secretary of Treasury.
2 *Appointment of the Comptroller:*	by President for 5-year term.
3 *Oath of the Comptroller:*	within 15 days of notice of appointment.
4 *Deputy Comptrollers:*	Secretary of Treasury designates no more than 4 • 1 designated First Deputy • exercise duties during Comptroller's disability/absence.
4a *Delegation of authority:*	permits Comptroller to delegate any power.
7 *Chief National Bank Examiner:*	Comptroller designates • chief of examining division.
8 *Clerks:*	Comptroller employs as necessary.
9 *Additional employees:*	Comptroller employs as necessary.

12 USC

10
Allocation of salaries: part of examining expenses.

11
Interest in national banks: prohibits for Comptroller and other officials.

12
Seal: Secretary of Treasury approves • filed with Secretary of State.

13
Office facilities: Treasury Department provides rooms and vaults.

14
Annual report: from OCC to Congress.

482
Employees of Office of the Comptroller of the Currency; appointment; compensation and benefits: exempts compensation from government pay scale consistent with other banking agencies.

15 USC

57a(f)
Unfair and deceptive practices by banks: FRB issues rules • requires OCC to establish a separate division of consumer affairs • OCC enforces rules • requires OCC to report to Congress on its activities March 15 of each year • permits banks to apply to FTC for exemption from any rule.

REGULATIONS

12 CFR

Part 4

Description of Office Organization, Procedures, Public Information: central office positions and field office structure • certain authority delegated to districts • examination/reporting process • catalogs all official OCC forms/ publications • instructions for public access to official papers, including Freedom of Information requests/ fees.

BANKING CIRCULARS

BC-205

OCC Staff No-Objection Positions: informal advisory letters • no precedents.

BC-239

Procedures for Certification of National Bank Documents: replaces BC-179.

2

GENERAL OCC SUPERVISORY AUTHORITY

STATUTES

12 USC

93
Violations of law; forfeiture; civil money penalties:

ensures due process before OCC and in court for violators (banks, directors, officers, employees, agents, et al.) • 3 tiers of penalties • covers "institution-affiliated parties" until 6 years after end of status.

93a
Authority to prescribe rules and regulations:

assigns responsibilities to OCC • prohibits general rulemaking for branching or securities activities of banks.

121a
Redemption of notes identifiable as to bank of issue:

OCC cancels and destroys redeemed notes.

161
Report of condition; call report:

covers bank resources and liabilities, payment of dividends, affiliates • permits OCC to require additional reports • requires publishing of reports in newspaper.

12 USC

164 *Penalty for failure to make reports:*	3 tiers of penalties: $2,000 per day for unintentional error/$20,000 per day for simple failure/lesser of $1,000,000 per day or 1% of assets per day for knowing or reckless failure • administrative hearings.
248(d) *Issue and retirement of Federal Reserve notes:*	FRB supervises and regulates through OCC.
418 *Federal Reserve notes:*	OCC and Secretary of Treasury have jurisdiction over plates and dies.
419 *Deposit of Federal Reserve notes:*	OCC controls deposit with and delivery by Treasury/Mint.
420 *Plates and dies:*	OCC controls • Federal Reserve Banks pay expenses.
421 *Examination of plates, dies, etc.:*	OCC examines Federal Reserve note materials.
481 *Examinations of national banks:*	OCC examines banks/affiliates as necessary • OCC compensates examiners • OCC examines foreign operations of state banks at FRB request • $5,000 per day penalty for affiliate defiance.

12 USC

482 *Employees of Office of Comptroller of Currency; appointment; compensation and benefits:*	exempts compensation from government pay scale consistent with other banking agencies • defrays examination expenses • proportionate to assets or resources • permits OCC to charge trust examination fees.
483 *Examination of member banks:*	FRB examines as necessary • permits FRB to assess costs of examinations.
484 *Visitorial powers:*	subjects banks to inspection only as authorized by law or Congressional directive • permits states to examine national bank records for compliance with unclaimed property or escheat laws.
486 *Waiver of reports from or examinations of affiliates:*	permits OCC or FRB to waive.
501a *Failure of national banks to comply with National Bank Act:*	bank forfeits franchise for violation of any provision (or for failure to become member bank after 1913) • U.S. District Court determines noncompliance upon suit by FRB under OCC direction.

12 USC

504

Civil money penalties:

permits OCC to impose for violations of insider transaction laws • 3 tiers of penalties: $5,000 per day for simple violation/$25,000 per day for reckless violation/lesser of $1,000,000 per day or 1% of assets for knowing violation • "institution-affiliated party" until 6 years after end of status.

1817(a)(2)-(3)

Report of condition:

permits FDIC access to examination/call reports • 4 call reports per year to OCC • 2 of 4 are basis for certified statement.

1818(a)(2)-(10)

Termination of insurance:

FDIC determines grounds and gives 30-day advance notice to OCC • FDIC gives notice to bank • FDIC holds hearing • FDIC publishes notice of termination • insurance continues from 6 months to 2 years • permits FDIC and OCC to suspend insurance at capital-deficient banks • prohibits delegation of FDIC authority to terminate.

12 USC

1818(b)-(l),(n),(u)-(v)
Cease and desist; removal of officer of director:

applies to banks/"institution-affiliated parties"/bank holding companies/foreign banks with domestic branches • temporary/permanent cease-and-desist orders • suspension/removal • judicial review • 3 tiers of civil money penalties • restraining orders against asset transfers • requires OCC to hold public hearings and publish written agreements/final orders unless contrary to public interest • permits OCC to assist/request assistance of/transfer information to foreign banking authorities.

1820(c)
Powers of examiner:

permits OCC personnel to administer oaths and examine into bank/affiliate affairs.

1829(c),(d)
Powers of examiner:

administers oaths • examines banks/affiliates on matters relating to affairs or ownership of banks.

1829b
Retention of records by insured banks:

Secretary of Treasury prescribes records to be maintained • requires maintenance for up to 6 years, except in special circumstances.

1831k
Reward for information leading to recoveries or civil penalties:

permits OCC with U.S. Attorney General to pay for original information yielding recoveries or forfeitures • limits reward to 25% of recovery ($100,000 maximum) • government officials and wrongdoers not eligible.

12 USC

1881-1884

Bank Protection Act of 1968: requires certain security measures for banks • OCC enforces/regulates • $100 per day penalty for violation of any rule.

1973-1978

Tie-in provisions: federal jurisdiction • subpoenas • treble damage suits • injunctive relief • 4-year statute of limitations • governs tying 1 bank service to another or making 1 service conditional on purchase of another service.

2255

Report of other banks and lending institutions: requires OCC on request to provide to FCA all information concerning banks doing business with Farm Credit System.

REGULATIONS

12 CFR

Part 19
Rules of Practice and Procedure:

applies to OCC adjudicative proceedings/formal investigations • appearance/practice before OCC • pleadings/motions/interlocutory review • party/nonparty participation • prehearing procedures • discovery/subpoenas • subjects formal hearings to Administrative Procedure Act • posthearing procedures • OCC initial/final decisions • cease-and-desist proceedings • assessment of civil money penalties • removals/suspensions/prohibitions • securities law proceedings • formal investigations under OCC supervisory powers • prescribes standards of conduct for parties/representatives/attorneys/accountants.

REGULATIONS (cont.)

12 CFR

Part 21
Minimum Security Devices and Procedures; Reports of Crimes and Suspected Crimes; Bank Secrecy Compliance:

minimum standards for security devices and procedures • requires banks to file compliance statements in June of odd-numbered years • requires banks to keep records of external crimes • special reports at request of OCC • $100 per day penalty for violation • requires banks to file Criminal Referral Forms (long or short form) for all crimes involving insiders; for crimes involving $1,000 aggregate loss where suspect is identified; mysterious loss of $5,000 (exemptions for robberies/ burglaries and for loss of securities where SEC report is filed) • requires filing within 30 days of detection of crime • failure to file reports may subject bank/officers/directors to civil money penalties • requires banks to develop compliance programs • minimum standards for content of program.

INTERPRETIVE RULINGS

12 CFR

7.6025(b),(c)
Books and records of national banks:

interprets 12 USC 484 visitorial powers • examination reports are confidential.

7.7540
Reports of condition; waiver of affiliate reports:

requires publication of affiliate report when report requested by OCC.

BANKING CIRCULARS

BC-57 (Revised)

Bank Holding Company Affiliates: requires bank to maintain copy of bank holding company annual reports/proxy statements.

BC-74; Supps. 1 & 2

Schemes to Defraud Involving Use of the Mails

BC-109; Supp. 1

Interagency EDP Examination Scheduling and Report Distribution Policy Statement: joint or rotated examinations of data centers • examination reports distributed to data centers.

BC-135

Fraudulent Use of Documents Purporting to be "ICC (International Chamber of Commerce) Notes": collateral for large financial transactions.

BC-152

OCC Banking Issuances: reference system.

BC-171; Supps. 1-133

Offshore Shell Banks: warning notices.

BC-174

Visitorial Powers of State Authorities: exception to 12 USC 484 for enforcement of state escheat laws.

BC-183

United States Dollar Traveler Express: warning.

BC-184

Window Dressing Official Call Reports: prohibits temporary transactions intended to realign balance sheet (12 USC 161).

BANKING CIRCULARS (cont.)

BC-186
Scheme to Obtain Financing for Bogus Insurance Policies.

BC-201
Allowance for Loan and Lease Losses.

BC-202
Accounting for Net Deferred Tax Charges.

BC-203 (Revised)
Accounting for the Costs for Internally Developed Computer Software.

BC-208; Supp. 1
Guidelines for Troubled Real Estate Loans; Clarification of Guidelines.

BC-211
South African Freeze: loans to South African Government.

BC-215
Guidelines for Collateral Evaluation and Classification of Troubled Energy Loans.

BC-217
Omnitek Intertrade Corporation; Spectrum-Guardian Management Trust.

BC-226
End-User Computing: information processing on microcomputers and small mainframes at bank • control of risks.

BANKING CIRCULARS (cont.)

BC-227 (Revised)

Standard Criminal Referral Forms: implements 12 CFR 21.11 • reporting of known/suspected crimes/mysterious disappearances/unexplained shortages/money laundering • Reportable Crimes and Losses Chart.

BC-229

Information Security: protection of information produced/stored/transmitted by computer • maintenance of confidentiality of all information.

BC-231

Basle Supervisors' Committee Statement on Principles of Money Laundering: international coordination • cross-reference to 12 CFR 21.21, Procedures for Monitoring Bank Secrecy Act Compliance.

BC-234

The Indiana National Bank, Indianapolis, Indiana: bogus cashier's checks and money orders.

BC-237

Annuity Contracts: warning of insolvency of American Teachers Life Insurance Company.

BC-243; Supp.1

Suspicious Transactions: illegitimate "Prime Bank Discounted Letters of Credit" and "Zero Coupon Letters of Credit" • "Insurance Binders" as backup collateral.

BC-246 (Revised)

Composite Ratings Definition: "CAMEL"/Consumer Compliance/CRA/Electronic Data Processing/Trust • reflects bank's condition/legal compliance/operating soundness.

3

ORGANIZATION AND CAPITAL STRUCTURE OF NATIONAL BANKS

STATUTES

12 USC

21 *Organization of national banks:*	5 or more organizers • requires drafting of articles of association • requires copy for OCC.
21a *Amendment to articles of association:*	by approval of majority of stockholders • requires 10-day prior notice of meeting • requires certified copy of amendment for OCC.
22 *Organization certificate:*	requires name, place, amount of capital, shareholders, banking purpose • requires "national" in name.
23 *Filing and preservation of organization certificate:*	requires court or notary acknowledgment/authentication and transmittal to OCC.
26 *Authorization to commence banking business:*	requires OCC to receive certificate, ensure that capital stock is paid-in, and adduce all other pertinent facts by taking sworn statement of directors.

12 USC

27
Certificate:

requires OCC to issue when it determines lawful entitlement to engage in banking • permits banks to be limited to exercising trust powers only • permits OCC to charter bankers' banks.

28
Publication of certificate:

in local newspaper for at least 60 days immediately following issuance.

35
Conversion of State banks into national banks:

permits any state bank with sufficient capital to convert by vote of 51% of shareholders and OCC approval • requires "national" in new name • permits OCC to permit retention of nonconforming assets.

51
Capital requirements:

sets minimum capital for localities of different sizes • requires paid-in surplus to equal at least 20% of capital.

51a
Preferred stock:

permits issuance on 51% vote of shareholders given 5 days' prior notice and after OCC approval • requires no notice/vote for new bank • stock not valid until par value paid-in, notice of sworn statement sent to OCC and certificate issued.

12 USC

51b-1

Capital impairment; preferred stock:

capital not impaired if valued at par or above • permits cumulative dividends after OCC approval of relevant articles of association.

51c

Common stock; capital; capital stock:

definitions.

52

Capital stock:

creation of shares • rights transferred when stock transferred • contents of stock certificates • requires certificates to be signed/sealed.

53

Capital stock required to commence business:

requires stock to be paid-in.

55

Assessments upon shareholders:

pro rata within 3 months after notice from OCC that stock is impaired • refusal by shareholder to pay triggers requirement to auction stock and publish newspaper notice.

56

Withdrawal of capital; dividends; bad debts:

prohibits withdrawal of capital generally • prohibits dividends if losses exceed undivided profits • prohibits dividends generally from exceeding net profits minus losses and bad debts.

12 USC

57 *Increase of capital; stock dividend:*	requires 2/3 vote of shareholders and OCC approval • requires sworn statement of president/cashier to be sent to OCC • requires OCC to issue certificate • permits stock dividends to be used to increase stock.
59 *Reduction of capital:*	requires 2/3 vote of shareholders and OCC approval • prohibits reduction below required minimum.
60 *Dividends:*	permits declaration quarterly, semiannually or annually out of net profits • establishes minimum surplus requirements • requires OCC approval when dividends for year exceed net profits plus retained net profits of preceding 2 years • defines "net profit".
62 *Shareholders list:*	requires accuracy/completeness • kept at bank office • permits inspection by shareholders, creditors, state tax officials • requires copy to be sent to OCC within 10 days of OCC request.
81 *Place of business:*	requires business to be transacted only in bank offices specified in organization/branch certificates.
143 *Reserves of nonmember national banks:*	requires 15% of deposit and circulating note amounts to be on hand at all times • applies only to banks not located in any state.

12 USC

144

Correspondent bank balances as reserves for nonmember banks: permits 4/5 of 15% required under 12 USC 143 to be in form of balances due from certain banks in Reserve cities.

221

Federal Reserve Act definitions: defines "bank," "national bank," "member bank," "board," "district" and "reserve bank."

222

National banks as member banks: requires FRS membership and FDIC insurance.

377

Affiliation with company engaged in distribution of securities: prohibits for member banks • penalty of $1,000 per day.

466

National banks outside continental U.S. as nonmember banks: permits FRS membership.

548

State taxation of national banks: requires treatment identical to state banks for tax purposes.

1814(b)

Certificate of OCC authorizing transaction of banking business: requires FDIC insurance • requires OCC to issue certificate to FDIC.

1816

Factors considered in issuing certificate to do business: FDIC looks at financial history/ condition of bank, capital structure, earnings prospects, character of management, risk to deposit insurance fund, convenience and needs of the community and lawfulness of corporate powers.

12 USC

1828(n)

Calculation of capital: prohibits bank from including goodwill acquired after 4/12/89.

3907

Capital adequacy (International Lending Supervision Act of 1983): permits OCC to establish minimum levels of capital for banks • capital below minimum is unsafe/unsound practice • enforceable under 12 USC 1818(b) • permits OCC to deny any proposed action affecting capital if it would impede bank plan to achieve minimum level.

REGULATIONS

12 CFR

Part 3
Minimum Capital Ratios; Issuance of Directives:

defines "Tier 1 capital," "Tier 2 capital," "Total capital," "Adjusted total assets" • previously purchased intangible assets remain partially includable in Tier 1 capital until 12/31/92 • requires bank to maintain minimum risk-weighted assets ratio and total assets leverage ratio • requires filing with OCC of plan to achieve minimum ratios • permits OCC to set higher minimum ratios for individual banks • OCC enforces with penalties/disciplinary actions • permits FDIC to terminate insurance for noncompliance • procedures for OCC to issue capital directives under 12 USC 3907 • Risk-Based Capital Guidelines (effective 12/31/90): capital components, risk categories/weights, transition rules/target ratios.

Interpretive Rulings: Capital and surplus.

Part 5, Subpart B (§§5.20-5.22, 5.24, 5.27)
Organization of a national bank; Organization of an interim national bank; Organization of a national bank limited to trust powers; Conversion; Organization of a national bankers' bank:

application process • filing fees • forms • prescribes procedures to implement statutes.

REGULATIONS (cont.)

12 CFR

Part 5, Subpart D
(§§5.46-5.47)
Changes in equity capital; Subordinated debt:

requires shareholder approval • requires OCC approval • administrative procedures • 12-month deadline for change/ issuance.

Part 28
(§28.6)
Capital equivalency deposits for Federal branches and agencies:

requires deposits to be kept at local member banks equaling greater of capital required of banks or 5% of liabilities of Federal branch • requires OCC approval to diminish deposits • requires ledger account.

INTERPRETIVE RULINGS

12 CFR

7.1100
Capital and surplus:

[superseded by 12 CFR Part 3].

7.6025(a)
Books and records of national banks; inspection:

restates access rules in 12 USC 62 and notes additional right of courts to inspect.

7.6040
Fractional shares:

suggests methods by which bank may avoid problems created by selling fractions of shares.

INTERPRETIVE RULINGS (cont.)

12 CFR

7.6100

Limitations on payment of dividends: restates rules in 12 USC 60 • requires regional approval if dividends will exceed net profits • restates rules in 12 USC 51b • prohibits dividend if bank has not paid FDIC assessment.

7.6120

Dividends payable in property other than cash: requires directors to get OCC approval • requires dividend equal to current value, even if property written off • prescribes bookkeeping procedures.

7.6125

Payment of dividends; bad debts: defines bad debt, including maturing/securing of debt • requires bank to document evaluation of security for bad debts and maintain on file.

BANKING CIRCULARS

BC-192

Organization Costs: accounting treatment (12 CFR 5.20).

BC-209

Dividends: continual analysis of capital position and annual update of comprehensive capital plans.

BC-212; Supps. 1 & 2

Capital Forbearance Policies: agricultural/oil and gas banks; temporary amendment to 12 CFR Part 32 creating substitute lending limit for certain national banks with charged-off agricultural or oil and gas loans; modification for banks with concentrations in weak economic sectors.

4

MANAGEMENT/SHAREHOLDER RIGHTS AND RESPONSIBILITIES

STATUTES

12 USC

51b
Rights and liabilities of preferred shareholders:

right to cumulative dividends/voting/control to extent articles of association permit after OCC approval • preferred shareholders not individually liable for bank debts, etc. • requires preferred shareholders to be paid before common shareholders.

61
Voting of national bank stock:

cumulative voting rights • permits voting by proxy • excludes stock held by the bank as sole trustee from determination of requisite number of shareholders for majority or 2/3 vote.

64a
Termination of double liability:

[obsolete: all requirements relate to statutes repealed in 1959].

66
Liabilities of fiduciaries:

trustees, executors, administrators, etc., not personally liable as shareholders • liability only for trusts, estates, etc.

71
Directors:

requires at least 5 directors • 1 year term • shareholders elect at meeting.

12 USC

71a

Number of directors:

5 to 25 • violation triggers 30-day OCC notice followed by appointment of receiver or conservator.

72

Qualifications of directors:

requires U.S. citizenship • requires 2/3 to reside in same state as bank or within 100 miles • permits OCC to waive citizenship requirement for minority of directors at bank affiliated with foreign bank • requires director to own $1000 par value stock or equivalent interest in bank or holding company.

73

Oath of directors:

requires swearing before notary that qualifications have been met and performance will be in good faith • transmittal to OCC.

74

Vacancy in board of directors:

other directors appoint substitute to hold office until next election.

75

Election of directors:

on day fixed in bylaws, within 60 days as fixed by directors or, after 10-day notice, on date fixed by 2/3 vote of shareholders.

76

President as director:

requires president to be member of board and chairman • permits directors to elect another member as chairman.

12 USC

78
Person engaged in underwriting as director:

prohibits except when FRB makes exception under its rules.

375
Purchases and sales involving directors:

permits only in regular course of business on nonpreferential terms • requires disinterested directors to authorize by affirmative vote • permits FRB to require full disclosure by director involved.

375a
Loans to executive officers:

no limits on loans for dwelling or education of children • permits other loans up to limit prescribed by regulator • requires officer to make written report to board on indebtedness to other banks above limits set for loans from officer's bank • permits officer to endorse/guarantee loans for protection of bank in good faith.

375b
Loans to executive officers, directors, and principal shareholders:

individual lending limit applies to the aggregate of insider's personal and business interests • prohibits insider loans above amount prescribed by regulator without prior board approval • requires loans to be on nonpreferential terms • prohibits overdrafts to directors/executive officers.

376
Interest on deposits of directors, officers, etc.:

prohibits preferential treatment.

12 USC

503

Liability of directors or officers:

knowing violation triggers personal liability for damages suffered by bank/shareholders.

1828(k)

Authority to regulate or prohibit certain forms of benefits to institution-affiliated parties:

FDIC may prohibit/limit "golden parachute"/indemnification payments by bank • prescribes determinative factors • prohibits prepayment by bank of liability/ legal expense if in contemplation of insolvency or as creditor preference • permits purchase by bank of commercial insurance policy/fidelity bond.

1829

Prohibition on control of or participation in depository institution by certain convicted persons:

requires institution-affiliated party to obtain prior FDIC written consent for crime involving dishonesty/ breach of trust • minimum 10-year prohibition period for violation of 18 USC 215, 656, 657, 1005, 1006, 1007, 1008, 1014, 1032, 1341, 1343, 1344, 1956 • permits court exception on motion by FDIC • $1,000,000 per day penalty.

1831i

Agency disapproval of directors and senior executive officers of insured depository institutions or depository institution holding companies:

requires bank to notify OCC 30 days before engagement of new director or senior executive officer • applies to new bank/bank with recent change-in-control/capital-deficient bank • permits OCC to disapprove • prescribes content of notice • prescribes standards for disapproval • OCC defines coverage.

12 USC

1831j

Depository institution employee protection remedy:

prohibits discharge of/ discrimination against "whistleblowers" giving information to OCC • permits employee to sue bank within 2 years • prescribes court remedies • excludes employees participating in wrongdoing/providing false information.

1972(2)

Certain correspondent account arrangements prohibited:

requires loans from correspondent banks to directors/officers/10% shareholders or their related interests to be nonpreferential • preferential loan arrangements bar bank from opening or maintaining a correspondent relationship • 3 tiers of civil money penalties • covers "institution-affiliated parties" for 6 years after end of status • requires insiders to report to board on loans from correspondent banks • permits OCC to impose additional reporting/disclosure rules.

3201-3207

Depository Institution Management Interlocks Act:

geographic/asset-size restrictions on interlocking directorates among banks • exempts interlocks with failing/failed depository institutions and holding companies • grandfathers most interlocks until 1993 • 15-month grace period for nongrandfathered interlocks that are prohibited due to change in circumstances.

15 USC

19
Interlocking directorates:

prohibits director/officer/employee of member bank from serving as director/officer/employee of any other bank or trust company except where certain degree of common ownership exists or in other limited circumstances.

79q(c)
Relationship with public utility holding companies:

prohibits bank management from serving as directors/officers of public utility holding companies.

80a-10(c)
Relationship with registered investment companies:

prohibits managers of any 1 bank from constituting majority of board of registered investment company.

REGULATIONS

12 CFR

Part 5, Subpart D (§5.51)
Changes in directors and senior executive officers:

implements 12 USC 1831i • defines "director" and "senior executive officer" • requires 30-day prior notice to OCC by new bank/bank recently undergoing change-in-control/capital-deficient bank • automatic approval if not disapproved • appeal procedure.

REGULATIONS (cont.)

12 CFR

Part 18

Annual Financial Disclosure to Shareholders:

applies to all banks except those subject to 12 CFR Part 11 or in holding companies • requires banks to notify shareholders of financial information availability • flexible format.

Part 26

Management Official Interlocks:

implements 12 USC 3201-3207 • permits OCC to approve interlock, if requested • permits OCC to shorten 15-month grace period for certain interlocks prohibited under changed circumstances • exempts interlocks at certain types of banks, or under circumstances endangering safety/soundness.

Part 31

Extensions of Credit to National Bank Insiders:

cites 12 USC 375a restriction on loans to executive officers • requires preapproval of certain loans to executive officers/directors/principal shareholders • disclosure on written request of executive officers/principal shareholders borrowing from correspondent banks • no disclosure of loans under $2,500 • 2-year recordkeeping of disclosure requests • FRB Regulation O (12 CFR Part 215) definitions apply • refers to 12 USC 1972(2) insider reports.

INTERPRETIVE RULINGS

12 CFR

7.4000 *Notice of shareholders' meetings:*	10-day notice by first-class mail • for consideration of certain actions, longer notice and certified mail.
7.4005 *Date of shareholders' meeting:*	specified in bylaws • restates 12 USC 71 • suggests text of fourth article for bylaws.
7.4010 *Quorum for shareholders' meeting:*	flexible • fixed in articles or bylaws or by general corporate law.
7.4020 *Director or attorney as proxy:*	permits • prohibits officers/clerks/tellers/bookkeepers as proxies.
7.4100 *Number of directors:*	5 to 25 • restates 12 USC 71a.
7.4105 *Annual meeting for election of directors:*	scheduled as close to fixed date as possible • directors serve until successors are elected.
7.4110 *Honorary directors or advisory board:*	permits appointment • no decision making authority.
7.4200 *Qualifications of directors:*	cites 12 USC 72.
7.4205 *Person convicted of crime serving as director, officer, or employee:*	cites 12 USC 1829.

INTERPRETIVE RULINGS (cont.)

12 CFR

7.4210 *Ownership of stock necessary to qualify as directors:*	restates 12 USC 72 • bank or holding company stock eligible • certain encumbrances on shares prevent their qualifying under statute.
7.4300 *Cumulative voting in election of directors:*	cites 12 USC 61 • example of how to cumulate votes.
7.4305 *Filling vacancy in or increasing board of directors:*	cites 12 USC 74 • if bank has 15 directors, permits directors to vote increase of 2 • if bank has 16 or more directors, permits increase by 4.
7.4400 *Organization meeting:*	after election returns come in, requires chairman or secretary to notify new directors to organize new board.
7.4410 *List of directors:*	requires board to send to OCC on prescribed form immediately after organization meeting.
7.4415 *Oath of Directors:*	restates 12 USC 73 • permits individual or joint oaths • transmittal to OCC.
7.4420 *Quorum of board of directors; proxies not permissible:*	prohibits directors from voting by proxy • requires quorum to be majority of full board.

INTERPRETIVE RULINGS (cont.)

12 CFR

7.4425 *Delegation of directors' duties:*	prohibits delegation of responsibility • permits assignment of performance.
7.5000 *Bonus and profit-sharing plans:*	permits any reasonable plan that insures adequate remuneration.
7.5010 *Pension plans:*	requires uniform treatment for all employees.
7.5200 *President as director:*	restates 12 USC 76 • requires president to be director • need not be chairman.
7.5210 *Same person holding offices of president and cashier:*	prohibits.
7.5215 *Fidelity bonds covering officers and employees:*	adequate coverage for all officers/ employees • criteria for adequacy.
7.5217 *Indemnification of directors and officers:*	permits except when individual adjudged guilty of willful misconduct, gross neglect of duty, or criminal acts.
7.5220 *Contracts of employment:*	restates 12 USC 24(5) reasonable terms/conditions.
7.5230 *Purchase of employee's residence:*	permits to facilitate transfer • requires bank to divest property early.

INTERPRETIVE RULINGS (cont.)

12 CFR

7.5245
Duties of cashier performed by secretary: permits if provided in bylaws.

7.6005
Restricting transfer of stock and record dates: permits bank to close records for short period near time of annual meeting to ascertain shareholders • alternatively, permits bank to fix record date.

7.6010
Facsimile signature on bank stock certificates: permits manual or facsimile signature of president/cashier.

7.6015
Lost stock certificates: if articles or bylaws establish no procedures, permits bank to follow state law in replacing certificates.

7.6050
Preemptive rights: requires articles to provide for, or specifically negate, vesting of rights in shareholders • requires 2/3 vote.

7.6060
Voting trusts: permits, if in conformance with state law.

BANKING CIRCULARS

BC-115; Supp. 1

Income Diversion through Management and Other Fees: requires satisfactory records demonstrating fair market value of services provided by management/shareholders and reasonableness of fees paid.

BANKING CIRCULARS (cont.)

BC-124

12 USC 72 Citizenship Requirement for Directors: waiver for foreign-owned bank.

5

GENERAL POWERS OF NATIONAL BANKS

STATUTES

2 USC

441b
Political contributions or expenditures:

prohibits bank from contributing to political campaigns or to labor organization • permits nonpartisan activities • permits bank to establish separate fund for political purposes supported by voluntary contributions from employees, shareholders, etc.

12 USC

24(1)-(6)
Corporate powers:

corporate seal • succession • contracts • sue/be sued • elect/appoint officers • adopt bylaws.

24(7)(first sentence)
Corporate powers:

necessary incidental powers • discount/negotiate notes, drafts, bills • receive deposits • buy/sell coin and bullion • lend money • circulate notes.

24(8)
Corporate powers:

permits bank to contribute to community funds/philanthropic instrumentalities.

24(9)
Corporate powers:

permits bank to issue/sell GNMA-guaranteed securities.

12 USC

24(10)

Corporate powers:

permits bank to invest up to 10% of assets in tangible personal property for lease/financing on net lease basis.

25a

Prohibited activities:

prohibits bank from involvement with any lottery • permits lawful banking services for state operating lottery.

92

National bank as insurance agent:

permits where population does not exceed 5,000 people • prohibits guarantee of premium payments.

94

Venue of suits against national banks in receivership and FDIC as receiver:

any Federal court in district where bank located • any state/municipal court in county/city where bank located.

265

Insured banks as depositaries of public money:

permits U.S. Treasury to deposit money with any insured bank • permits bank to act as financial agent of U.S. • requires bank to post satisfactory security for deposits • prohibits U.S. from favoring any type bank over another.

374

Member bank as agent of nonmember bank:

prohibits member bank from applying for discounts from Federal Reserve Bank on behalf of nonmember bank without permission from FRB.

12 USC

463
Limitation on amount of balance with any depository institution without access to Federal Reserve advances:

prohibits member bank from depositing with nonmember bank more than 10% of capital/surplus.

3401-3420
Right to Financial Privacy Act of 1978:

bank records confidential • prohibits government authority from obtaining bank customer records unless customer notified in advance • permits bank to notify government of possible violation of law • permits Federal agencies to transfer bank customer records to Attorney General • permits customer to challenge in court • restricts use of information • civil penalty against banks/government for violation • exceptions for government investigations/ supervisory examinations/law enforcement proceedings • permits Federal banking agencies and SEC to exchange information freely • suspends statute of limitations on any matter during court challenge by customer • prohibits bank personnel from disclosing information in grand jury subpoena.

28 USC

1348
Jurisdiction of district courts in actions involving national banks:

grants U.S. District Courts original jurisdiction when U.S. sues any bank or when civil action involves receivership of bank.

1394
Action by national bank to enjoin the Comptroller of the Currency:

permits bank to bring suit in its own judicial district.

REGULATIONS

12 CFR

Part 2
Disposition of Credit Life Insurance Income:

prohibits bank insiders/employees from benefiting personally from sale of credit life insurance • requires all shareholders to benefit equally • permits crediting income to bank affiliate • permissible insurance sales methods • permits offering incentives/bonuses to employees • permits bank to apply to OCC for modification of rules.

INTERPRETIVE RULINGS

12 CFR

7.3500
Use of data processing equipment and furnishing of data processing services:

permits bank to perform for itself/ others all banking services in automated fashion.

7.7010
National bank as guarantor or surety on indemnity bond:

permits, if bank has substantial interest in performance of the transaction.

7.7100
National banks acting as general insurance agents:

restates 12 USC 92 • permits any office of bank to sell insurance if located in community of 5,000 or less, even if other offices not so located.

7.7200
Authority to act as "finder":

permits bank to accept fee for bringing together buyer and seller • prohibits further involvement.

INTERPRETIVE RULINGS (cont.)

12 CFR

7.7315
Charging additional fee for credit report or investigation of borrower: permits except where barred by state statute law.

7.7430
Preparing income tax returns for customers or public: permits with or without fee.

7.7445
Charitable foundations: permits bank to establish under specified conditions • requires disclosure of operations to OCC • limits contributions to 5% of pretax income.

7.7479
Charitable contributions: permits when directors authorize • limits to 5% of pretax income.

7.7482
Postal service by national banks: permits bank to run postal substation and earn income from operation • requires separate books for inspection by U.S. Postal Service.

7.7490
Messenger service: permits armored car service if agreement between bank and customer designates messenger as agent of customer • some state laws may limit messenger arrangements.

INTERPRETIVE RULINGS (cont.)

12 CFR

7.7500
Sale of money orders at nonbanking outlets: permits bank to designate bonded agents to sell its money orders away from bank • signature of bank officer indicates bank accepts draft with issuance • absence of signature indicates ordinary draft subject to presentment.

7.8000
Charges by banks: requires each bank to fix charges/ fees independently • prohibits agreement or discussion with other banks • lists factors to be considered in fixing charges • preempts state law limiting charges • defers to 12 CFR for fiduciary accounts and 12 CFR 7.7515 for dormant accounts.

BANKING CIRCULARS

BC-58 (Revised); Supp. 1

Coin and Bullion: authority and guidelines for transactions (12 USC 24(7)).

BC-137

Prohibition on Political Contributions by National Banks: elections/primary elections/political conventions/caucuses (2 USC 441b).

BC-151

Payment of Membership and Other Fees to Associations Which Discriminate on a Prohibited Basis: joint agency policy statement.

BANKING CIRCULARS (cont.)

BC-168

Charges by a Federal Reserve Bank Against a National Bank's Reserve Account Due to a Default on a Loan Made to a Nonmember Financial Institution: Reserve Account Charge Agreements • prohibits irrevocable charge as illegal binding guarantee • permits revocable charge (12 CFR 7.7010).

BC-177 (Revised)

Contingency Planning for Electronic Data Processing Support.

BC-187

Financial Information on Data Processing Servicers.

6

CORPORATE STRUCTURE/ACTIVITIES OF NATIONAL BANKS

STATUTES

12 USC

30
Change of name or location:

permits name change without OCC approval • requires name to include "national" • permits change of location of main office to any authorized branch within same municipality • requires 2/3 shareholder vote/OCC approval for move beyond municipality (up to 30 miles).

31
Effect of changes of name:

all debts/rights/powers remain same.

32
Effect of change of name or location:

no release of bank from liability • no effect on any legal action.

36
Branches:

permits branches to be retained after conversion to national charter or after merger • requires OCC to approve branches • state law controls conditions for establishing branches • definition of "branch" (deposits received, checks paid or money lent).

12 USC

95
Limitations during emergency periods; designation of legal holiday for national banks:

permits President to declare emergency and order banks to cease or limit business • $10,000 fine for violation • permits OCC to designate any day as legal holiday for banks • permits banks to close if state or state official declares holiday for state banks.

214
Conversion, merger or consolidation Statewise:

definitions.

214a
Conversion, merger or consolidation Statewise:

requires 2/3 shareholder vote • requires plan of conversion, merger or consolidation to be published in local newspaper • permits OCC to waive publication on request • permits dissenting shareholders to have stock appraised • permits appeal of valuation to OCC.

214b
Termination of franchise:

automatic upon conversion • resulting state bank has same obligations as former bank.

214c
Limitations on conversion or consolidation or merger of national banks into or with State banks:

state law governs transaction • permits conversion into bank without state approval.

12 USC

215
Consolidation:

requires OCC to approve • requires 2/3 shareholder vote • requires newspaper notice to precede vote • entitles dissenting shareholders to appraisal of stock • involves OCC in appraisal • consolidated bank has same rights/obligations as predecessor banks • frees stock of consolidated bank from former shareholder preemptive rights.

215a
Merger

requires OCC approval • requires 2/3 shareholder vote • requires newspaper notice to precede vote • entitles dissenting shareholder of merged bank to appraisal of stock • involves OCC in appraisal • frees stock of acquiring bank from former preemptive rights of merged bank shareholders.

215b
Consolidation and merger definitions:

defines "state bank," "state," "Comptroller" and "receiving association."

221a
Affiliates:

defines "affiliate" • affiliate owns more than 50% of member bank or is owned more than 50% by member bank • actual control qualifies irrespective of shares held.

1814(c),(d)
Continuation of insurance:

FDIC insurance continues when state bank converts to national charter and vice versa • FDIC insurance continues when insured banks merge/consolidate.

12 USC

1817(j)

Changes in control of bank:

requires 60-day prior notice to OCC • permits OCC to extend review period • permits OCC to veto • permits request of hearing if change denied • U.S. Court of Appeals reviews OCC denial • prescribes information for notice to OCC • requires OCC to prepare written report • requires OCC to publish names of applicants and to seek public comment • OCC and U.S District Court enforce compliance • 3 tiers of civil money penalties • covers "institution-affiliated parties" until 6 years after end of status • excludes transactions under Bank Holding Company Act/Bank Merger Act/ Savings and Loan Holding Company Act.

1828(c)

Merger, consolidation, or takeover by insured banks:

requires prior written OCC approval • requires newspaper notice to precede consummation • requires consideration of antitrust/ managerial aspects • requires 30-day advance notice to U.S. Attorney General • emergency approval provisions • requires OCC annual report to Congress on mergers.

1828(i)(2)

Conversion of national bank into insured bank:

requires OCC approval of conversion of District of Columbia bank if capital stock or surplus will be diminished.

12 USC

1841-1850

Bank Holding Company Act of 1956 (As Amended): holding company has actual control over bank or owns 25% of bank's stock • presumes no control below 5% • defines "bank" as FDIC-insured or institution accepting demand deposits and making commercial loans • exceptions • requires FRB to approve acquisitions of banks by holding companies • standards for approval • prohibits acquisition across state lines except where state statute law permits • permits holding company to hold only entities that are closely related to banking • permits holding company to acquire savings institutions • prohibits general insurance activities • requires companies to register with FRB • criminal penalties • 3 tiers of civil money penalties • covers "institution-affiliated parties" until 6 years after end of status [*See* FRB Regulation Y: 12 CFR Part 225].

REGULATIONS

12 CFR

Part 5, Subpart A (§§5.1-5.14)
Rules of General Applicability:

corporate filings with OCC • application forms/procedures • delegates certain authority to OCC district offices • filing fees • establishes public files • hearing requests/rules • requires OCC to notify applicants of decisions • refers to sample forms in *Comptroller's Manual for Corporate Activities.*

Part 5, Subpart C (§§5.30-5.31, 5.33-5.34)
Expansion of Activities:

OCC considers certain factors in branch/customer-bank communication terminal (CBCT) applications • preliminary approvals expire in 9 months • filing fees • application procedures/factors considered for merger, consolidation and purchase/assumption • application/notice procedures for domestic operating subsidiaries (80% owned by bank).

Part 5, Subpart D (§§5.40, 5.42, 5.50)
Other Changes in Activities and Miscellaneous Activities:

application/notice procedures for changes in location • application fee • notice procedures for change of corporate title • notice procedures for change in bank control.

REGULATIONS (cont.)

12 CFR

Part 8
Assessment of Fees; National Banks, District of Columbia Banks, Federal Branches and Agencies: semiannual • charges interest on delinquent payments at Treasury current value of funds (TFRM) rate.

INTERPRETIVE RULINGS

12 CFR

7.5015
Employee stock option and stock purchase plans: permits banks to provide.

7.7115
Insuring lives of bank officers: permits "key man" insurance if death would have significant consequences for bank.

7.7434
Business hours: requires hours to be fixed by bank independently • prohibits arrangements with other banks or clearinghouses.

7.7516
Sharing of banking quarters: permits if 2 institutions are clearly identified as separate for customer purposes • permits officers/employees to perform services for both institutions under proper agency agreements.

BANKING CIRCULARS

BC-175
Legal Bank Holidays: cites 12 USC 95 and 12 CFR 7.7434.

BC-189
Branch Closings and Reductions in Service.

BC-199
Loan Production Offices.

BC-230
Merger Procedures: corporate reorganization • streamlined approval preceding shareholder approval • disclosure of OCC approval to shareholders.

BC-232
Procedures for Processing Notices of Change in Bank Control - Voting Trusts and Banks in Organization: no interpretation of prior notice requirements under 12 USC §1817(j).

BC-236
Quasi-Reorganization: application procedures • cites 12 USC §§56,59,60 • sample balance sheet.

BC-240
Push Down Policy: accounting for bank acquisitions • sample illustration.

7

SECURITIES ACTIVITIES OF NATIONAL BANKS

STATUTES

15 USC

78b *Necessity for regulation:*	protects interstate commerce, national credit, and federal taxing power • increases effectiveness of banking system • ensures maintenance of fair/honest markets.
78c *Definitions and application of title:*	defines actors in securities field • defines "statutory disqualification" with respect to participation in self-regulatory organization (e.g., securities exchange).
78i *Manipulation of security prices:*	prohibits use of mails or any instrument of interstate commerce to create false appearance of active trading and affect the price of any security or to induce purchase or sale • personal liability of violators • 3-year statute of limitations.
78j *Manipulative and deceptive devices:*	prohibits use of mails or any instrument of interstate commerce to effect a short sale, stop-loss order or other deceptive device.

15 USC

78l

Registration requirements for securities:

prohibits dealing in unregistered securities on a national securities exchange • requires application to be made with exchange/SEC • requires certain information in application • registration effective 30 days after exchange approves and certifies to SEC • permits SEC to exempt securities • OCC regulates bank securities with "substantially similar" rules.

78m

Periodical and other reports:

requires securities issuers to file current information/annual reports with SEC • SEC prescribes report forms • requires issuers to keep accurate books/records • criminal liability for knowing circumvention of internal controls/falsification of accounts • requires 5% equity security holder to file information on personal background and intent to control with SEC/issuer/exchange • filing fees • requires institutional investment managers to file reports with SEC at least annually • permits SEC to exempt issuers/managers • requires manager banks to file with banking agency/SEC.

15 USC

78n
Proxies:

requires reports to shareholders to be made at time of management proxy solicitation • requires reports to be filed with SEC • requires tender offers for more than 5% of securities to be accompanied by report to SEC • prohibits misrepresentation of material facts • requires report to shareholders/SEC when person acquiring securities intends to elect majority of directors at other than shareholders' meeting.

78o(c)(4), (d)
Registration and regulation of brokers and dealers:

SEC enforces compliance with registration/report • requires securities issuers to file periodic updated reports with SEC.

78o(f)
Prevention of misuse of nonpublic information:

requires written policies/procedures to safeguard material nonpublic information • SEC issues rules.

78o-4
Municipal securities -- Registration of municipal securities dealers:

prohibits manipulation of municipal securities trading • requires dealers to register with SEC • 120-day approval process • establishes Municipal Securities Rulemaking Board (MSRB) • OCC supervises bank municipal securities dealers • SEC supervises MSRB • permits MSRB to require limited reports.

15 USC

78o-5

Government securities brokers and dealers:

prohibits government securities transactions by unregistered brokers/dealers • requires banks to file notice with OCC of status as broker/dealer • requires OCC to share notice filings with SEC • prescribes broker/dealer registration procedures with SEC • Treasury Department issues rules and exemptions in consultation with FRB and SEC • grants SEC enforcement powers • OCC enforces for unregistered/exempted bank brokers/dealers with notice to SEC • permits OCC to examine records of bank brokers/dealers • requires registered broker/dealer membership on national securities exchange • prohibits SEC from investigating brokers/dealers supervised by OCC.

78p

Directors; Officers and principal stockholders:

requires reports of beneficial ownership interests by directors, officers and 10% shareholders to be filed monthly or periodically with SEC/exchange • profits from insider information belong to issuer • requires securities sold to be transferred within 20 days and to be owned by seller.

15 USC

78q

Records and reports -- Rules and regulations:

SEC prescribes records to be kept and disseminated by exchanges, dealers, securities associations, transfer agents and clearing agencies • permits SEC to require any reports necessary • permits SEC to rely on self-regulatory organizations for supervision • requires brokers/dealers to file annual financial statements with SEC • permits SEC to delegate its authority to OCC for banks • FRB regulates credit extensions by brokers/dealers.

78q-1

National system for clearance and settlement of securities transactions -- Congressional findings; facilitating establishment of system:

SEC or banking regulator registers clearing agencies according to certain standards • registration of transfer agents • requires SEC and banking regulators to consult/ coordinate supervision of clearing agencies/transfer agents.

78r

Liability for misleading statements:

permits person misled by misrepresentation of material facts to sue perpetrator as personally liable • 3-year statute of limitations.

78t

Liabilities of controlling persons:

person controlling anyone who violates securities laws is personally liable • prohibits anyone to delay filing of any required report • person purchasing/selling securities with material nonpublic information is liable to seller/purchaser.

15 USC

78t-1
Liability to contemporaneous traders for insider trading:

permits private court action against traders possessing material nonpublic information • limits damages recoverable • 5-year statute of limitations • imposes liability for communication of information.

78u
Investigations and actions -- Authority and discretion of Commission to investigate violations:

grants SEC broad investigative authority on own behalf or for foreign authorities • subpoena power • permits SEC to seek injunction in U.S. District Court against imminent violations • self-regulatory organizations ordinarily enforce their own rules • prohibits consolidation of SEC court action with other private court actions.

78u-1
Civil penalties:

permits SEC to prosecute traders using material nonpublic information • maximum penalty of treble profits • limits liability of controlling persons • SEC issues exemptions • collection procedures • 5-year statute of limitations • permits bounties to informants.

78w
Rules, regulations and orders; annual reports:

grants full regulatory authority to SEC, FRB, OCC and FDIC within their respective jurisdictions • requires agencies to report annually to Congress on work in securities field.

15 USC

78x

Public availability of information:

requires all securities filings to be disclosed under Freedom of Information Act (5 USC 552).

78aa

Jurisdiction of offenses and suits:

U.S. District Court in district where violation occurred or where defendant lives or does business.

78bb

Effect on existing law -- Addition of rights and remedies; recovery of actual damages; State securities commissions:

commissions charged by brokers/dealers not unlawful merely because they exceed commissions charged by others • permits regulatory agencies to prescribe disclosure of commissions policies/ practices.

78dd-1

Foreign corrupt practices by issuers:

prohibits registered securities issuer or management or agent of issuer from making payments to foreign officials to influence business transactions • exception for routine governmental action • permits citation of foreign laws or *bona fide* business expenditures as affirmative defense • Attorney General issues guidelines and opinions.

15 USC

78dd-2
Foreign corrupt practices by domestic concerns:

prohibits nonissuer person or person's management or agent from making payments to foreign officials to influence business transactions • exception for routine governmental action • permits citation of foreign laws or *bona fide* business expenditures as affirmative defense • Attorney General issues guidelines and opinions • fines and prison terms.

78ff
Penalties:

up to $1,000,000 fine/10 years imprisonment for any violation of securities laws by natural person • up to $2,500,000 fine for violation by nonnatural person • up to $2,000,000 fine for violation of 15 USC 78dd-1 (foreign corrupt practices) by an issuer • up to $100,000 fine/5 years imprisonment for officers/directors/stockholders/ employees of issuer.

REGULATIONS

12 CFR

Part 10
Municipal Securities Dealers:

application procedures for municipal securities principals/ representatives • refers to MSRB rules • Forms MSD-4/MSD-5.

REGULATIONS (cont.)

12 CFR

Part 11
Securities Exchange Act Disclosure Rules

Subpart A -- General Provisions

11.101
Scope of Part: applies to all securities subject to registration under Sections 12(b) or 12(g) of Securities Exchange Act of 1934.

11.102
Definitions: defines fundamental terms • distinguishes types of subsidiaries.

11.103
Filing of material with Comptroller of the Currency: in Washington, D.C.

11.104
Inspection: in Washington, D.C. • registration statements/annual reports in District Office.

11.105
Nondisclosure of certain information filed: procedure for requesting confidential treatment.

11.106
Liability for forward-looking statements: assumes statements made on reasonable basis in good faith • affects quarterly reports (Form F-4) and annual reports • defines "fraudulent statement".

REGULATIONS (cont.)

12 CFR

11.107
Falsification of accounting records:

refers to book/record/account subject to Section 13(b)(2)(a) of Securities Exchange Act of 1934.

11.108
Bank's representations in connection with the preparation of required reports and documents:

prohibits materially false/misleading statement by director/officer to accountant • prohibits causing third person to omit material fact.

11.109
Notice of adjudication:

prompt notice by OCC of adverse action/final disposition • requires written reasons.

Subpart B -- Registration

11.201
Requirement of registration statement under Section 12 of the Exchange Act; exemption from registration:

refers to Sections 12(b) and 12(g) and Forms F-1 and F-10 • exempts 90-day warrants • exempts bank with assets up to $3,000,000.

11.202
Registration of securities of successor bank:

requires securities of acquired bank to be registered following merger/ consolidation/securities exchange/ asset acquisition with registered bank • requires acquiring nonregistered bank to file timely registration statement for acquired registered bank • exempts securities held by less than 300 persons.

REGULATIONS (cont.)

12 CFR

11.203

Registration effective as to class or series: refers to Sections 12(d) and 12(g)(1) of Exchange Act.

11.204

Acceleration of effectiveness of registration: requires bank and/or exchange to request in writing with reasons.

11.205

Exchange certification: form of certification by exchange • amendment • withdrawal • registration of security not terminated if trading suspended.

11.206

When securities are deemed to be registered: upon effectiveness of registration statement.

11.207

Deregistration: requires compliance with Section 12(d) of Exchange Act and rules of the exchange for securities registered on national exchange • requires certification by bank to OCC of below 300 holders, or 500 holders with assets up to $3,000,000 for securities registered under 12(g) of Exchange Act • effective after 90 days.

Forms

11.290

Form for registration of securities of bank pursuant to Section 12(b) or Section 12(g) of the Securities Exchange Act of 1934 (Form F-1).

REGULATIONS (cont.)

12 CFR

11.291

Form for registration of additional class of securities of a bank under Section 12(b) or Section 12(g) of the Securities Exchange Act of 1934 (Form F-10).

11.292

Form for amendment to registration statement or periodic report of bank (Form F-20).

Subpart C -- Annual and Other Bank Reports

11.301

Requirement of annual report and annual reports of predecessors:

requires conformity with Form F-2 • requires every bank to file annual report for each predecessor with securities registered under Section 12 of Exchange Act.

11.302

Exception from requirement of annual report:

requires no annual report if registration statement initially effective during annual report filing period.

11.303

Current reports:

requires conformity with Form F-3 • requires filing within 15 days of reportable event.

REGULATIONS (cont.)

12 CFR

11.304

Quarterly reports: requires conformity with Form F-4 • requires filing within 45 days after end of quarter.

Forms

11.390

Form for annual report of a bank (Form F-2).

11.391

Form for current report of a bank (Form F-3).

Subpart D -- Transactions by Certain Shareholders

11.401

Requirement of acquisition statements pursuant to Section 13(d) or Section 13(g) of the Exchange Act: requires report by person acquiring 5% of any class of equity security registered under Section 12 of Exchange Act • requires conformity with Form F-11 • permits Form F-11A as alternative • requires filing with OCC within 10 days after acquisition • permits joint filing by group of individual acquirors.

11.402

Amendments to acquisition statements: required for any material change in facts reported on Form F-11 or Form F-11A.

11.403

Determination of beneficial ownership: defines "beneficial owner".

REGULATIONS (cont.)

12 CFR

11.404

Disclaimer of beneficial ownership: permits declaration that any filing is not admission of beneficial ownership under Sections 13(d), 13(g), 14(d) of Exchange Act.

11.405

Acquisition of securities: subjects beneficial owner of securities to Sections 13(b), 13(g), 14(d) of Exchange Act.

11.406

Exemption of certain acquisitions: exempts acquisition of securities by person owning more than 5% of same class of securities from Section 13(d) of Exchange Act.

11.410

Reports of directors, officers and principal stockholders pursuant to Section 16(a) of the Exchange Act: requires preparation in filing of statements in conformity with Form F-7/Form F-8 • method of determining 10% ownership • permits disclaimer of beneficial ownership • treatment of securities held in trust • treatment of presently exercisable puts/calls/options/obligations to buy/sell securities • exempts odd-lot transactions • exempts securities transactions under $10,000 over 6-month period • 12-month exemption for executors/administrators/guardians/committees/receivers/bankruptcy trustees/assignees/conservators/liquidating agents • authorizes OCC to exempt • exempts acquisitions/dividend reinvestment.

REGULATIONS (cont.)

12 CFR

11.411

Exemption of certain transactions from Section 16(b) of the Exchange Act:

investment company transactions • distribution of substantial block of securities • acquisition of stock/stock options/stock appreciation rights under certain specified plans • sale/purchase of securities pursuant to exercise of option/warrant/right not acquired within 6 months • disposition of securities pursuant to binding merger/consolidation/acquisition plan • disposition of securities pursuant to bank holding company formation • certain voting trust/deposit agreements • conversion of securities • certain subscription rights.

11.412

Exemption of certain securities from Section 16(c) of the Exchange Act:

over-allotment/offset sale by dealer • sales of securities to be acquired • certain arbitrage transactions • securities orders executed by disinterested broker.

Forms

11.490

Acquisition statement filed under Section 13(d) of the Exchange Act (Form F-11).

11.491

Short form acquisitions/ownership statement to be filed under Section 13(d) or Section 13(g) of the Exchange Act (Form F-11A).

REGULATIONS (cont.)

12 CFR

Forms (cont.)

11.492

Statement of beneficial ownership of equity securities filed under Section 16(a) of the Exchange Act (Form F-7).

11.493

Statement of changes in beneficial ownership of equity securities to be filed under Section 16(a) of the Exchange Act (Form F-8).

Subpart E -- Shareholder Meetings

11.501

Requirement of proxy/information statement: requires conformity with Form F-5.

11.502

Exceptions: solicitation of less than 10 persons • solicitation by person for securities in own/nominee's name or in own custody without remuneration, with all soliciting material and with impartiality • solicitation by beneficial owner • solicitation by advertisement • advising business associates.

REGULATIONS (cont.)

12 CFR

11.503

Annual report to security holders to accompany statements:

covers annual meeting with directors' election • requires 1 report per address • report content and format • transmittal to OCC.

11.504

Requirements as to proxy:

requires identification of bank or nonmajority solicitor/date/subject matter • format for notation of choices/votes • conditions for discretionary voting authority.

11.505

Presentation of information in statement:

content/format of proxy.

11.506

Material required to be filed:

requires transmittal to OCC of proxy/information statements 10 days before distribution (15 days if not routine) • requires additional transmittal to OCC for annual meeting with changes from previous year noted • requires transmittal to OCC of additional soliciting material 2 days in advance • requires transmittal of final statement to OCC upon distribution • requires transmittal of all materials for personal solicitation 5 days in advance • requires transmittal to OCC of definitive copies of other materials upon distribution • format for revised materials • filing effective upon receipt by OCC.

REGULATIONS (cont.)

12 CFR

11.507

Mailing communications for security holders:

requires bank management to provide certain information on request during proxy solicitation • method of soliciting brokers/dealers/trustees/nominees holding securities of record.

11.508

Proposals of security holders:

requires inclusion in proxy statement if proponent is eligible (as defined) • requires proponent to give proper notice and attend or be represented at meeting • requires proponent to submit proposal sufficiently in advance • requires proponent to make single proposal • requires 500-word supporting statement to be included on proponent's request • permits bank to omit proposal if inappropriate for action, in violation of law, contrary to SEC rules, redresses personal grievance, affects less than 5% of bank's operations, *ultra vires,* affects conduct of ordinary bank business, concerns election to office, counters concurrent proposal by bank, is moot/duplicative, repeats proposal previously submitted for vote or concerns specific dividend amounts • requires advance transmittal to OCC and proposal of plan to omit and reasons • requires bank to give proponent advance notice of inclusion of opposition statement • permits proponent to contest opposition with OCC.

REGULATIONS (cont.)

12 CFR

11.509

False or misleading statements: prohibits with respect to material facts/omissions • disclaims OCC certification of truth.

11.510

Prohibition of certain solicitations: undated/postdated/imprecisely dated proxy.

11.511

Special provisions applicable to election contests: solicitation opposing solicitation relating to election/removal of directors • requires advance filing with OCC/securities exchanges in conformity with Form F-6 • conditions for furnishing security holders with Form F-6 before proxy statement issuance • filing requirements.

11.512

Solicitation prior to furnishing required proxy statement: permits if in opposition to prior solicitation with preemptive effect, no form of proxy furnished, solicitors fully identified and written proxy statement follows • filing requirements.

Forms

11.590

Form for proxy and information statement (Form F-5).

11.592

Form for statement in election contests (Form F-6).

REGULATIONS (cont.)

12 CFR

Subpart F -- Tender Offers

11.601 *Scope and definitions applicable to Subpart F (the "Tender Offer Regulations"):*	requires tender offers to comply with Section 14(d)(1) of Exchange Act, including affiliate tender offers.
11.602 *Commencement of a tender offer:*	starting event • distinguishes between public/other announcements • tender offer not commenced by certain communications.
11.603 *Filing and transmittal of tender offer statement:*	requires filing of Form F-13 for bid for over 5% of class of securities • requires transmittal of filing notice to subject bank/other bidders/ securities exchanges/NASD.
11.604 *Dissemination of certain tender offers:*	conditions for materials to be deemed "published or sent or given to security holders" under Section 14(d)(1) of Exchange Act • requires prompt dissemination of material changes.

REGULATIONS (cont.)

12 CFR

11.605

Obligations of the subject bank and bidder:

requires bank to notify transfer agents/others upon receipt of bidder's written request • requires bank to prepare current shareholder list • requires bank to make election whether or not to comply with request • requires bank to mail tender offer materials to shareholders or deliver shareholder lists to bidder if compliance elected • clears bank of liability for solicitation/underwriting • content of bidder's request • requires bidder to make election whether or not to require bank to disclose material changes • requires bidder to defray bank's expenses • requires bidder to mail tender offer materials to security holders on request • requires bidder to restrict use of shareholder lists to dissemination of tender offer materials.

11.606

Disclosure requirements with respect to tender offers:

requires publication at commencement • use of shareholders lists/security position listings • requires post-commencement advertisement and publication • requires prompt disclosure of material changes.

REGULATIONS (cont.)

12 CFR

11.607 *Additional withdrawal rights:*	permits withdrawal within 15 business days after commencement or within 10 business days after commencement of competing tender offer • content/timeliness of withdrawal notice.
11.608 *Pro rata rights:*	applies to tenders of less than all of outstanding securities of a class.
11.609 *Solicitation/recommendation statements with respect to certain tender offer statements:*	requires transmittal to OCC of Form F-12 • notice to securities exchanges/ NASD at time of first publication or distribution • requires certain information • covers certain persons • exempts "stop-look-and-listen" communications by bank • covers statement of management's position.
11.610 *Unlawful tender offer practices:*	requires tender offer to remain open 20 business days • prohibits increase in offered consideration or soliciting fee unless open additional 10 business days • requires payment of consideration or return of deposited securities • prohibits extending length of tender offer without notice.
11.611 *Position of subject bank with respect to a tender offer:*	requires disclosure within 10 business days • requires disclosure of material changes.

REGULATIONS (cont.)

12 CFR

11.620

Restrictions on control persons: defines "control person" • requires control person to file statement with OCC describing securities purchases.

11.630

Change in majority of directors: requires securities acquirors to give advance notice to OCC/other securities holders of intent to elect/designate.

Forms

11.690

Tender offer statement to be filed pursuant to Section 14(d)(1) of the Exchange Act (Form F-13).

11.691

Solicitation/recommendation to be filed under Section 14(d)(4) of the Exchange Act (Form F-12).

Subpart G -- Requirements Concerning Registration and Reporting

11.701

Scope of subject: registration statements/reports of registered banks.

11.702

Title of securities: requires indication of type/general character of securities.

REGULATIONS (cont.)

12 CFR

11.703 *Supplemental information:*	authorizes OCC to request • requires return to registrant upon request.
11.704 *Interpretation of requirements:*	clarifies nature of information sought on forms.
11.710 *Requirements as to proper form:*	assumes use of proper form • permits OCC to object within 30 days.
11.711 *Number of copies; signatures; binding:*	transmittal to OCC • manual signatures • stiff covers.
11.712 *Requirements as to paper, printing and language:*	requires 8½" x 11" white paper • roman type • English.
11.713 *Preparation of statement or report:*	requires numbers/captions of all items (text optional) • requires inapplicable/negative answers to be noted.
11.714 *Riders, inserts:*	prohibits riders • permits full insert pages.
11.715 *Amendments:*	requires separate amendments for each form • refers to Form F-20.
11.720 *Additional information:*	requires for avoidance of misleading statements.

REGULATIONS (cont.)

12 CFR

11.721
Information unknown or not available: requires showing of reasonable effort, expense or nonaffiliation with person possessing information.

11.722
Disclaimer of control: requires bank to state pertinent material facts.

11.723
Incorporation by reference and summaries or outlines of documents: permits • requires satisfaction of requirements of form/report in which incorporated • refers to Rule 24 of SEC Rules of Practice.

11.724
Notification of inability to file timely annual or quarterly report or portions thereof: requires transmittal to OCC of Form 12b-25 within 1 business day after due date.

11.730
Additional Exhibits: permits as bank desires.

11.731
Omission of substantially identical documents: permits schedule identifying omitted documents • requires detail of material differences among documents.

11.732
Incorporation of exhibits by reference: covers documents previously filed • requires statement of subsequent modifications • prohibits reference to documents filed more than 5 years previously (except charter/ bylaws).

REGULATIONS (cont.)

12 CFR

Subpart H -- Content of Non-Financial Statements and Reports

11.800 *General:*	annual reports, proxy/information statements and other documents filed under Exchange Act.
11.811 *Description of business:*	requires detail.
11.812 *Description of Property:*	requires detail.
11.813 *Pending legal proceedings:*	requires detail.
11.821 *Market price and dividends on the bank's common equity and related shareholder matters:*	requires detail.
11.822 *Description of bank's securities:*	requires detail.
11.831 *Selected financial data:*	requires detail.
11.832 *Supplementary financial information:*	requires detail.
11.833 *Management's discussion and analysis of financial condition and results of operations:*	requires detail.

REGULATIONS (cont.)

12 CFR

11.834 *Disagreements with former accountants on accounting and financial disclosure:*	requires detail.
11.841 *Directors and executive officers:*	requires detail.
11.842 *Executive compensation:*	requires detail.
11.843 *Security ownership of certain beneficial owners and management:*	*requires detail.*
11.844 *Certain relationships and related transactions:*	requires detail.
11.861 *Exhibits:*	requires detail.
11.871 *Recent sales of securities:*	requires detail.
11.872 *Indemnification of directors and officers:*	requires detail.

REGULATIONS (cont.)

12 CFR

Subpart I -- Financial Statement Requirements

11.900 *General rules:*	requires financial statement verifications to include date/manual signature/place of issuance/ portions covered • requires exceptions/qualifications to be specifically stated.
11.901 *Definitions:*	defines "associate" and "ordinary course of business".
11.902 *Opinions to be expressed by principal accounting officer and internal auditor:*	identifies accounting principles • consistency of application.
11.903 *Examination by independent public accountants:*	OCC recognizes independence • statement about auditing procedures • extent of accountant's opinions/exceptions • reliance on other accountants.
11.910 *Verification requirements:*	requires verified statements.
11.911 *Consolidated financial statements:*	requires for bank and its significant subsidiaries.
11.912 *Analysis of changes in equity capital:*	requires reconciliation of balances • note or separate statement.

REGULATIONS (cont.)

12 CFR

11.913 *Age of financial statements and mailing date of proxy or information statement:*	requires update within 135 days of mailing date • special rules for mailing near end of fiscal year.
11.914 *Instructions to income statement requirements:*	requires reconciliation of total/net income for recently acquired businesses • requires affirmation of adjustments for fair presentation of nonverified statements.
11.915 *Financial statements of business acquired or to be acquired:*	requires filing for certain periods • requires verified statements for fiscal years • special rules for consolidated statements.
11.916 *Separate statements of unconsolidated subsidiaries and other persons:*	requires if material to understanding condition of total enterprise.
11.917 *Interim financial statements:*	permits condensed format.
11.918 *Filing of other statements in certain cases:*	grants discretion to OCC.
11.919 *Schedules to be filed:*	balance sheet schedules • income statement schedules • requires examination by independent public accountant.
11.920 *Principles of financial reporting:*	requires conformance with GAAP • requires accrual accounting.

REGULATIONS (cont.)

12 CFR

11.921 *Requirements as to form:*	whole dollars or thousands of dollars • negative amounts.
11.922 *Items not material:*	separate presentation not required.
11.923 *Inapplicable caption and omissions of unrequired or inapplicable financial statements:*	requires statement of reasons for omission.
11.924 *Additional information:*	as required for clarity.
11.925 *Reacquired evidences of indebtedness:*	requires deduction from liabilities.
11.926 *Foreign activities:*	requires separate disclosure • content of disclosures.
11.927 *Leased assets and lease commitments:*	requires application of Financial Accounting Standards No. 13.
11.928 *General notes to financial statements:*	specifies items.
11.929 *Principles of consolidation or combination:*	prefers consolidated statements.

REGULATIONS (cont.)

12 CFR

11.930
General instructions: financial statement formats • permits alternative reference to Article 9 of SEC Regulation S-X.

11.931
Balance sheet: refers to Consolidated Report of Condition • specifies caption/items.

11.932
Statement of income: refers to Consolidated Report of Income • specifies caption/items.

11.933
Schedules: prescribes 5 schedules.

11.940
Presentation requirements: circumstances requiring *pro forma* financial information.

11.941
Preparation requirements: form/content of *pro forma* financial information.

11.942
Presentation of financial forecast: permits substitution for *pro forma* condensed statements of income.

Part 16
Securities Offering Disclosure Rules: requires filing of offering circular with OCC • exempt transactions • optional abbreviated forms for smaller banks • defines exempt nonpublic offerings • form/content of offering circulars for existing bank and bank in organization • advertising restrictions.

REGULATIONS (cont.)

17 CFR

240.17f-1

Requirements for reporting and inquiry with respect to missing, lost, counterfeit or stolen securities:

requires bank to register with SEC • requires bank to report criminal theft/loss to SEC and transfer agent within 1 business day and to FBI promptly • requires bank to report noncriminal loss to SEC and transfer agent within 1 business day if missing for 2 business days • permits delayed reporting under certain circumstances • requires bank to report counterfeit securities to SEC, transfer agent and FBI within 1 business day • limited reporting by transfer agents • requires bank to report recovery of reported losses to SEC, transfer agent and FBI within 1 business day • specifies reportable information and forms • requires bank other than transfer agent/ registrar to ask SEC about securities certificates held • recordkeeping for 3 years.

REGULATIONS (cont.)

17 CFR

Part 400

Regulation of government securities brokers and dealers under the Government Securities Act of 1986:

Rules of General Application (§§400.1 - 400.6)

applies to banks • Treasury Secretary issues exemptions/interpretations • requires broker/dealer associated with bank to file specified forms with bank • requires broker/dealer bank to obtain forms from associated broker/dealer and file with OCC within 10 days • requires filing of amended information within 30 days on specified form • requires bank to notify OCC of termination of status as broker/dealer • termination effective 60 days after filing or as set by OCC.

Exemptions (§§401.1 - 401.8)

U.S. Savings Bond agents • bank purchasing U.S. Treasury securities for customers • bank handling less than 500 brokerage transactions annually/performing ministerial functions • bank dealing as fiduciary or through repurchase transactions • certain corporate credit unions • foreign bank branch/agency transacting broker/dealer activities outside U.S. • broker/dealer terminated by 10/31/87.

REGULATIONS (cont.)

17 CFR

Part 400 (cont.)

Financial Responsibility (§§402.1 - 402.2d)

not applicable to bank subject to OCC capital regulations and to foreign bank branch/agency regulated by OCC • special rules for futures commission merchants and government securities interdealer brokers • fixes and prescribes computation formulas for capital requirements for government securities brokers/dealers and affiliates.

Protection of Customer Securities and Balances (§§403.1 -403.7)

permits alternative compliance by registered broker/dealer with SEC rules • modifies 17 CFR Part 240 for hypothecation of government securities and use of customer free credit balances • modifies 17 CFR Part 240 for broker/dealer custody of government securities and customer rights • special rules for custody of government securities by broker/dealer banks • applies to futures commission merchants • all rules effective by 1/31/88 • prescribes disclosures to customers.

REGULATIONS (cont.)

17 CFR

Part 400 (cont.)

Recordkeeping and Preservation of Records (§§404.1 - 404.5)

permits alternative compliance by registered broker/dealer with 17 CFR Part 240 • modifies 17 CFR Part 240 for proof of money balances, computation of capital and details of clearing transactions • extends 17 CFR Part 240 to nonresident (outside U.S.) government securities brokers/ dealers • modifies 17 CFR Part 240 for preservation of records • defers to 12 CFR Part 12 for bank and foreign bank branch/agency • requires bank to keep special ledger for government securities and prescribes other forms • requires preservation of ledger for 6 years and forms for 3 years • modifies securities count rules under 17 CFR Part 240.

Reports and Audit (§§405.1 - 405.4)

exempts broker/dealer bank subject to OCC financial reporting rules • refers to recordkeeping and reporting requirements under 31 CFR Part 103 (Bank Secrecy Act regulations).

REGULATIONS (cont.)

17 CFR

Part 400 (cont.)

Forms

§449.1

Form G--FIN, Notification by financial institutions of status as government securities broker or dealer pursuant to §15C(a)(1)(B)(I) of the Securities Exchange Act of 1934.

§449.2

Form G--FINW, notification by financial institutions of cessation of status as government securities broker or dealer pursuant to §15C(a)(1)(B)(I) of the Securities Exchange Act of 1934 and §400.6 of this chapter.

§449.3

Form G--FIN-4, notification by persons associated with financial institutions that are government securities brokers and dealers pursuant to §15C(a)(1)(B)(I) of the Securities Exchange Act of 1934 and §400.4 of this chapter.

REGULATIONS (cont.)

17 CFR

Part 400 (cont.)

§449.4

Form G--FIN-5, notification of termination of association with a financial institution that is a government securities broker or dealer pursuant to §15C(a)(1)(B)(I) of the Securities Exchange Act of 1934 and §400.4 of this chapter.

§449.5

Form G--405, information required of registered government securities brokers and dealers pursuant to §15C of the Securities Exchange Act of 1934 and §§405.2 and 405.3 of this chapter.

REGULATIONS (cont.)

17 CFR

Part 400 (cont.)

Custodial Holdings of Government Securities by Depository Institutions (§§450.1 - 450.5)

applies to bank as fiduciary/ custodian/otherwise for account of customer and not broker/dealer • exempts banks covered by OCC fiduciary regulation and examination • prescribes standards for possession and control • prescribes procedures for handling FRB claims against customer securities • requires separate records for customer securities • requires record preservation for 6 years.

INTERPRETIVE RULINGS

12 CFR

7.4015
Solicitation of proxies for shareholders' meeting:

12 CFR Part 11 applies to banks with 500 or more shareholders • owner of convertible capital debenture is not equity security holder until conversion right has been exercised.

7.7530
Issuance of promissory notes:

permits bank to issue at par or discount • 12 CFR Part 16 applies to public note offerings.

BANKING CIRCULARS

BC-38; Amend. 1

Securities and Exchange Commission Rule 10b-17: notice to NASD of publicly traded securities distributions.

BC-98 (Revised); Supps. 1-3

Foreign Restricted List Issued by the SEC: foreign companies offering their securities in U.S. in violation of SEC registration requirements.

BC-176

Filing Review Procedures: annual reports/proxy materials/tender offers/insider trading reports.

BC-213

Timely Filing of Reports Under the Securities Exchange Act of 1934 and 12 CFR Part 11: OCC institutes enforcement actions or lawsuits for violations.

BC-223

Compliance with 12 CFR 16.5 Notice of Non-Public Sale: bank securities.

BC-245

SEC Financial Institution Task Force: bank holding company disclosure compliance • OCC securities disclosure enforcement program.

BC-247

Application of Securities Laws to Common Trust Funds: registration requirements of 15 USC 77a and 15 USC 80a-1 cover bank common trust funds lacking "*bona fide* fiduciary purpose".

8

ASSET/INVESTMENT POWERS OF NATIONAL BANKS

STATUTES

12 USC

24(7) (except first sentence)
Corporate powers and investment securities:

permits bank only to buy/sell securities on order of customer • permits bank to purchase investment securities for its own account under OCC rules • permits investment in securities of single obligor not to exceed 10% capital/surplus • prohibits ownership of stock in any corporation • designates eligible securities • permits investment of 10% of capital/surplus up to 5% of any class of voting securities of bankers' bank • permits investment in Canadian government obligations.

29
Authority to hold real estate:

permits bank to own bank premises • permits acquisition of property securing debts previously contracted • 5-year limitation • permits OCC to grant up to 5 more years if good faith attempt is made to dispose of property or if disposal would harm bank • permits bank to spend funds with OCC approval to develop/improve property held • limited exception for long-held land and subsurface rights.

12 USC

83
Purchase of own shares; loans secured by own shares:

prohibits except to secure debt previously contracted • requires disposal within 6 months if bank purchases own shares.

84
Lending limits:

limits unsecured loans to single borrower to 15% capital/surplus • permits loans secured by readily marketable collateral up to an additional 10% • excepts certain loans from general limits.

85
Interest charged:

permits bank to charge interest at greater of maximum rate allowed by its state or 1% over Federal Reserve discount rate • permits interest to be taken in advance.

86
Usury:

requires bank that knowingly charges more than interest rate ceiling to forfeit all interest • requires bank to return double the interest to borrower if interest already has been paid • 2-year statute of limitations.

371
Real estate loans:

permits banks to make, subject to OCC conditions • permits notes for construction of residential or farm buildings, maturing within 9 months and accompanied by firm take-out, to be discounted as commercial paper.

12 USC

371c

Loans to affiliates:

overall limit to 1 affiliate of 10% capital/surplus • overall limit to all affiliates of 20% capital/surplus • prohibits purchase by bank of low-quality asset from affiliate • defines "affiliate", "control" and "covered transaction" • requires 100% collateral if U.S. Government obligations; 110% if state/municipal obligations; 120% if other debt instruments; 130% if stock, leases, real or personal property • excepts loans to 80%-owned subsidiary • excepts certain transactions • FRB issues rules/additional exemptions.

371c-1

Restrictions on transactions with affiliates:

prohibits favored treatment of affiliates by bank/subsidiaries • applies to 12 USC 371c "covered transactions", sale of securities, payment of money/services, agency/ brokerage transactions, affiliate-related third-party transactions and transactions benefiting affiliates • prohibits certain purchases of affiliate securities/assets or affiliate-underwritten securities • prohibits bank from advertising its responsibility for affiliate obligations • FRB issues rules/ exemptions.

371d

Investment in bank premises:

prohibits aggregate of all such investments from exceeding 100% of bank's capital stock except with OCC approval.

12 USC

372 *Acceptance of drafts or bills of exchange:*	permits in foreign/domestic transactions if draft has no more than 6 months' sight to run • prohibits bank from accepting from 1 person more than 10% capital/surplus • aggregate limitation of 150% capital/surplus • permits FRB to authorize aggregate 200% • permits 50% of all acceptances to be related to domestic transactions • FRB defines/interprets.
373 *Acceptance of drafts for furnishing dollar exchange:*	permits as required by usages of trade in various countries if draft has no more than 3 months' sight to run • 10% capital/surplus overall limit • 50% limit with adequate security.
374a *Member bank as agent of nonbanking entity:*	prohibits bank from acting as agent of nonbank in making loans secured by investment securities to securities brokers/dealers • $100 per day fine for violation.
378 *Securities dealers and others engaging in the business of receiving deposits:*	prohibits after 6/16/34 (companion prohibition to 12 USC 24(7) barring banks from dealing in securities) • criminal penalties • permits persons or institutions authorized by state law and subject to examination/regulation to take deposits.

12 USC

582

U.S. notes as security: prohibits bank from offering or receiving U.S. notes or bank notes as security for loan (limited amount of U.S. notes remain in circulation and resemble other forms of paper currency).

1454

Mortgages of Federal Home Loan banks: permits insured bank to sell mortgage loan to FHLMC if loan-to-value ratio does not exceed 80% or if excess is insured by qualified loan insurer.

1701j-3

Due-on-sale clauses: requires lenders to enforce due-on-sale clauses in real estate loan contracts • creates 3-year window period of nonenforceability for clauses in contracts by lenders in states which enacted prohibitions • permits OCC/states to change rules for "window period" loans.

1709-1a

Effect of State legal limits on interest charged: exempts from state usury laws FHA/VA-insured loans secured by 1-to-4 family dwellings or to interim construction financing.

1718(f)

Purchase of stock of Federal National Mortgage Association: permits banks to own stock in FNMA.

12 USC

1730(l)(2)

Loans secured by stock; Reporting requirements:

requires president/CEO of insured bank to report to FDIC any loan bank makes secured by 25% or more of stock of federally insured financial institution • excepts stock held more than 1 year by borrower prior to loan or stock of new bank before opening.

l735f-7 (note)

Exemption from state usury laws:

permits federally insured depository institutions to charge interest or fees without limitation on loans secured by first lien on residential property or on stock in residential cooperative housing corporation • applies to mobile home loans under conditions established by FHLBB (now OTS) • permits subsequent state law (enacted by 4/1/83) to override.

1817(j)(9)

Loans secured by depository institution stock:

requires lender bank president to report to regulator of bank whose stock is collateral, if collateral is 25% or more of outstanding voting stock • exempts stock owned for 1 year or more/stock of new bank preopening.

1817(k)

Extensions of credit to bank insiders:

permits OCC to issue regulations requiring reporting/pubic disclosure of loans to executive officers/ principal shareholders/related interests.

12 USC

1831b

Limitations and disclosures with respect to certain federally related mortgage loans:

prohibits bank from making loan to agent or trustee without knowing identity of beneficial owner • permits FDIC to request report on identity of beneficial owner and nature of loan.

1831g

Contracts between depository institutions and persons providing goods, products, or services:

prohibits if contract performance would adversely affect safety/ soundness • FDIC issues rules • OCC enforces for banks • no private right of action • requires U.S. Attorney General report to Congress.

1861-1867

Bank Service Corporation Act:

permits bank to invest in a single bank service corporation (BSC) up to 10% capital/surplus and up to 5% of its total assets in all BSCs • prohibits BSC from excluding any depository institution from services • permits BSC to perform for banks and other persons "bank services" and other services permitted by FRB under §4(c)(8) of Bank Holding Company Act • subjects BSC to OCC examination • requires bank to notify OCC within 30 days of entering into service contract.

12 USC

1971-1972(1)
Tie-in provisions:

definitions • prohibits bank from lending money, leasing property, furnishing services, or fixing consideration for a loan, lease or service on the condition that customers partake of other bank services or forego business with competing banks • permits FRB to make exceptions.

3801-3805
Alternative Mortgage Transaction Parity Act of 1982:

requires state-chartered institutions to offer alternative mortgage instruments (AMIs) • defines "AMI" • requires OCC to identify regulatory provisions applicable to state banks • subsequent state law may override.

15 USC

682(b)
Small business investment companies (SBICs):

permits banks to own stock in SBICs up to 5% capital/surplus.

38 USC

1802(f)
Loans guaranteed by the Veterans Administration:

permits bank to make VA loans irrespective of limitations on loan-to-value ratio, loan maturity or real estate loan aggregate amount.

REGULATIONS

12 CFR

Part 1

Investment Securities Regulation: defines eligible securities (Type I unrestricted; Type II unrestricted but subject to 10% capital/surplus limits; Type III subject to 10% limit and restricted to purchase/sale) • requires maintenance of adequate credit information to demonstrate prudence • requires convertible securities to be written down to investment value • excepts securities acquired through foreclosure on collateral.

Part 5, Subpart C (§5.35)

Bank service corporations: ermits bank to invest up to 10% of its paid-in/unimpaired capital and its unimpaired surplus in bank service corporation (BSC) • permits bank to invest up to 5% of its total assets in BSC • requires OCC approval to invest in BSCs • requires OCC decision on proposed investment within 90 days • conditions for approval • authorizes OCC examination/supervision of BSC where bank is principal investor.

Part 5, Subpart C (§5.36)

Other equity investments: requires bank to submit letter to OCC District Office • 30-day review/ automatic approval • permits OCC to impose conditions.

REGULATIONS (cont.)

12 CFR

Part 12

Recordkeeping and Confirmation Requirements for Securities Transactions:

requires certain items concerning purchase/sale of securities for customers to be kept on file 3 years • requires certain items to be included in notice to customer when transaction accomplished • requires banks to establish written policies/ procedures • provides exceptions for banks with minimal number of transactions • permits OCC to make exceptions.

Part 32

National Bank Lending Limits:

cites 12 USC 84 • prescribes rules for combining loans to separate borrowers • permits noncombination of certain foreign loans • clarifies exceptions.

Interpretive Rulings: Obligations of accommodation parties; Sale of Federal funds; Purchase of securities subject to repurchase agreement; Purchase of third-party paper; Overdrafts; Loans charged off in whole or in part; Sale of loan participations; Interest or discount on loans; Loans to or guaranteed by general obligations of a state or political subdivision; Loans to industrial development authorities; Separate limitations for 12 USC 24 and 12 USC 84.

REGULATIONS (cont.)

12 CFR

Part 34

Real Estate Lending:

cites 12 USC 371 • permits banks to make, arrange, purchase or sell loans secured by real estate free from limits on loan-to-value, amortization, maturity, aggregate amount and certain leasehold terms • preempts state law • defines non-real estate loans • permits banks to make/acquire loan secured by lien on real property that includes due-on-sale clause (excepts certain transfers) • permits banks to make adjustable-rate mortgages (ARMs) • requires bank to relate ARM interest rate to index beyond bank control • permits prepayment fees on ARMs • requires consumer credit ARMs to include limit on maximum interest rate • requires consumer credit ARMs to include disclosures required by Truth-in-Lending Act regulations (FRB Regulation Z: 12 CFR Part 226) • certain provisions optionally applicable to state banks • preempts state law • prescribes real estate appraisal standards for federally related transactions • requires appraisals by state certified appraiser for transactions of $1,000,000/ nonresidential transactions of $250,000/complex residential transactions of $250,000 • requires appraisals by state licensed appraiser for transactions over $50,000 • exceptions • requires appraiser independence.

INTERPRETIVE RULINGS

12 CFR

7.3000
General authority: cites 12 USC 29.

7.3005
Real estate necessary for accommodation in the transaction of business: permits bank to hold real estate other than that on which bank buildings are located • permits bank to hold real estate for future bank premises.

7.3010
Municipal parking lots: recognizes expenditures to acquire parking facilities as business expense.

7.3020
Real estate acquired as salvage on uncollectible loans: permits bank to retain property for use in its business or transfer to subsidiary/affiliate • permits bank with OCC regional approval to arrange to receive additional compensation from transferee when real estate ultimately disposed.

7.3025
Other real estate owned (OREO): cites 12 USC 29 • requires bank to maintain documentation of diligent efforts to dispose of OREO • appraisal procedures • requires annual independent appraisal.

INTERPRETIVE RULINGS (cont.)

12 CFR

7.3100

Investment in bank premises or stock of a corporation holding premises:

permits bank/affiliate/subsidiary to hold directly • permits bank premises corporation to own fixed assets • requires OCC regional approval for investment greater than bank's capital stock • usual approval of fixed assets up to 50% of capital stock.

7.3300

Leasing of public facilities:

permits bank to build municipal building or school and lease to municipality • requires ownership to devolve to municipality at expiration of lease.

7.3400

Leasing of personal property:

permits under certain conditions, including requirement that lease be a net, full-payout lease representing noncancellable obligation of lessee • full-payout calculations • subjects leases to limitations under 12 USC 84, 371c • recognizes rights of bank to protect its interest in leased property.

INTERPRETIVE RULINGS (cont.)

12 CFR

7.6030
Purchase of own shares or loan secured by own shares:

cites 12 USC 83 • permits bank to require borrower to agree not to assign shares, to pledge shares when necessary and to leave shares in bank's custody • prohibits bank from making loans secured by its own notes/debentures.

7.7015
Check "guaranty" plans:

recognizes as essentially an agreement to extend credit to depositor • recognizes as legitimate bank power.

7.7016
Letters of credit:

permits bank to issue under Uniform Commercial Code or Uniform Customs and Practice for Documentary Credits • definite term/amount • bank's obligation to pay only upon presentment • unqualified obligation of customer to reimburse bank.

7.7310
Charging interest at rates permitted competing institutions; charging interest to corporate borrowers:

permits bank to lend at maximum state rate for any class of loans • permits bank to lend to corporate borrower at any rate agreed where state law denies usury defense to corporations.

INTERPRETIVE RULINGS (cont.)

12 CFR

7.7312
Loan agreement providing for share of profits, income or earnings: permits in lieu of interest • prohibits substitution for payment of principal.

7.7360
Loans secured by stock or obligations of an affiliate: exempts loans otherwise adequately secured from 12 USC 371c limitations if additional security taken in the form of affiliate stock/obligations.

7.7365
Federal funds transactions between affiliates: permits, subject to 12 USC 371c limitations.

7.7378
Issuance of credit cards: permits directly or through subsidiary.

7.7379
Servicing of mortgage and other loans as agent: permits directly or through subsidiary.

7.7380
Loans originating at other than banking offices: permits under Federal branching laws (12 USC 36, 81) if loans approved at bank office.

7.7420
Acceptances: permits banks to make unlimited variety of acceptances in financing credit transactions.

INTERPRETIVE RULINGS (cont.)

12 CFR

7.7455
National banks holding collateral stock as nominee:

permits bank to have stock it holds as loan collateral transferred to its name as nominee.

7.7480
Investments in community development projects:

permits banks to treat investment as charitable contribution • permits bank to treat as asset if project predominantly civic in nature and investment not in excess of 2% in single project/5% in all projects.

7.7495
Debt cancellation contracts:

permits arrangement of additional charges/reserves to allow cancellation of debt upon death of borrower.

7.7505
Accelerated depreciation for tax purposes:

permits bank to use accelerated procedure for tax purposes at same time it uses nonaccelerated method for financial accounting purposes.

7.7535
Receipt of stock from SBIC:

permits bank to receive stock dividends/other benefits of stock ownership from SBIC without violating stock purchase prohibition under 12 USC 24(7).

INTERPRETIVE RULINGS (cont.)

12 CFR

7.7570

Separate investment security limitations: permits application of 10% limit under 12 USC 24(7) separately to each security issue of single issuer under certain conditions.

7.7590

Interest rate escalation clause: permits in loan agreement under ordinary rules of contract law.

BANKING CIRCULARS

BC-21; Supps. 1 & 2

National Corporation for Housing Partnerships and National Housing Partnerships: permits investment in common stock/limited partnership interests (12 USC 24(7)).

BC-78

Exception to Lending Limits for OPIC Insured Standby Letters of Credit Issued by National Banks.

BC-79 (3rd Revision)

National Bank Participation in the Financial Futures and Forward Placements Markets: relates to commercial banking activities • can reduce interest-rate risk.

BC-105

Income Tax Remittance to Holding Company Affiliates: transfer of deferred income taxes from bank to affiliate is unsafe/unsound • constitutes loan to affiliate under 12 USC 371c.

BC-111 (Revised)

Acquisition or Use of Computer Systems: voluntary notice to and advance consultation with OCC • restates Bank Service Corporation Act (12 USC 1865) reporting requirements.

BANKING CIRCULARS (cont.)

BC-125
Leasing of Personal Property -- Interpretative Ruling 7.3400.

BC-127
Uniform Agreement on the Classification of Assets and Appraisal of Securities Held by Banks: distinguishes between investment and subinvestment quality securities.

BC-157
Retail Repurchase Agreements.

BC-169
Federal Home Loan Mortgage Corporation (FHLMC) Swap Program: accounting treatment.

BC-181 (Revised)
Purchases of Loans in Whole or in Part: participations (18 USC 641, 1005, 1014; 12 CFR 4.18(c)).

BC-182
Issuance of "Due Bills" to Customers Purchasing Securities (15 USC 78j; 12 CFR Part 12).

BC-185
Community Development Corporation and Investment Program: (12 CFR 7.7480) • eligibility of investments • OCC review process.

BC-191
Agricultural Credit Documentation.

BC-195
Accounting for Restructured Loans and Sales of Foreclosed Property: "troubled" debt restructurings/sales of OREO.

BC-196
Securities Lending: investment securities from bank's portfolio • loans to broker-dealers.

BANKING CIRCULARS (cont.)

BC-197
Premiums on U.S. Government Guaranteed Loans: SBA and FHA programs.

BC-199
Loan Production Offices.

BC-200
Accounting for Loan Swaps: foreign borrowers/financially troubled countries.

BC-201
Allowance for Loan and Lease Losses.

BC-208; Supp. 1
Guidelines for Troubled Real Estate Loans; Clarification of Guidelines.

BC-210
Repurchase Agreements: credit policies/prudent management procedures for control of securities collateral.

BC-211
South African Freeze: loans to South African Government.

BC-214
Debt Adjustment Program and Interest Rate Buy-Down Program: Farmers Home Administration programs to reduce risk in agricultural loan portfolio.

BC-215
Guidelines for Collateral Evaluation and Classification of Troubled Energy Loans.

BC-216
Securities Denominated in Foreign Currencies: subjects acquisition authority to 12 USC 24(7) and 12 CFR Part 1.

BANKING CIRCULARS (cont.)

BC-220

National Bank Investment in Investment Companies Composed Wholly of Bank Eligible Investments: 12 USC 24(7).

BC-221

Farm Products Lien: requires compliance with state security perfection requirements and Federal Food Security Act of 1985 (7 USC 1631).

BC-225

Real Estate Appraisals: uniform guidelines for internal policies/standards.

BC-228

Selection of Securities Dealers and Unsuitable Investment Practices: procedures for selecting advisors on bank investment portfolio management • objectionable investment activities.

BC-242; Supp. 1

Definition of Highly Leveraged Transactions (HLTs): joint agency action to promote uniform reporting of HLT exposures • qualifying tests and delisting criteria.

BC-248

Sale of Loans into the Federal Agricultural Mortgage Corporation ("Farmer Mac") Program.

9

LIABILITY POWERS OF NATIONAL BANKS

STATUTES

12 USC

90 *Financial agents of the government; depositaries of public money:*	permits banks to perform agency and depositary functions • requires satisfactory security • requires Treasury Secretary to apportion deposits equitably across nation • permits bank to hold state/local funds.
371a *Payment of interest on demand deposits:*	prohibits • permits automatic withdrawals by check from savings and transfer to demand accounts.
371b *Rate of interest on time and savings deposits:*	permits FRB to issue rules governing advertisement of interest in consultation with FDIC/FHLBB (OTS).
371b-1 *State usury ceilings inapplicable to obligations of banks and affiliates:*	(repealed 3/31/80: remains effective for deposits/obligations previously made) • prohibits bank or affiliate or its endorser, surety, guarantor, or assignee from raising defense of usury in connection with its deposits/obligations.
501 *Certification of checks:*	prohibits bank director/officer/employee/agent from certifying check without money on deposit to cover payment • penalties.

12 USC

1813(l)
International banking facility deposits:

include obligations payable outside U.S. • refers to FRB Regulation D (12 CFR Part 204).

1813(m)
Insured deposit:

amount due depositor up to $100,000, subject to FDIC regulations • includes deposits in U.S. branch of foreign bank payable in U.S., subject to FDIC regulations.

1831f
Brokered deposits:

prohibits acceptance by troubled bank • permits FDIC to waive prohibition • exception for banks in conservatorship • FDIC issues rules.

1832
Prohibition on certain activities by depository institutions:

permits NOW accounts only for individual and certain non-profit organizations • $1,000 fine for each violation.

2501-2503
Disposition of Abandoned Money Orders and Traveler's Checks:

permits state where purchased to escheat funds • permits state where bank located to escheat funds if state where purchased not known • permits bank's state to escheat if state of purchase has no escheat law.

12 USC

4001-4010

Expedited Funds Availability Act: effective 9/1/88, requires next business day availability for deposits of cash/wire transfers/government checks/certain other checks • effective 9/1/88 permits 2-day hold on local checks/proprietary automated teller machine (ATM) deposits and 6-day hold on nonlocal checks • effective 9/1/90, requires 1-day hold on local checks and 4-day hold on nonlocal checks • until 9/1/90 permits 6-day hold on local/nonlocal checks for non-proprietary ATM deposits • permits longer holds for new accounts and check deposits over $5,000 • FRB issues rules/exceptions for reasonable suspicion of uncollectability • permits FRB to temporarily suspend this Act for certain classifications of checks to prevent fraud losses • requires bank to disclose funds availability policy before account opened • requires bank to give notice to customers on deposit slips and at teller stations/ATMs • FRB designs model disclosure forms • requires bank to pay interest on interest-bearing account from business day of provisional credit • prohibits freezing of funds in account not subject to check hold • pre-9/89 law requiring shorter check holds supersedes this Act • OCC enforces for national banks • civil liability of bank for violation of this Act (actual damages plus dollar limits for individual/class actions) [*See* FRB Regulation CC: 12 CFR Part 229].

INTERPRETIVE RULINGS

12 CFR

7.7000
Guaranty or endorsement of notes or other obligations sold by the bank: permits for obligations it sells for own account.

7.7355
Debts of affiliate as bank indebtedness: recognizes affiliate obligations as bank obligations only where bank is obligor or guarantor • recognizes affiliate bad debts as bad debts of bank only for operating subsidiaries.

7.7370
Interest-bearing deposits between affiliated banks: recognizes as loan to affiliate subject to 12 USC 371c • prohibits bank from making interest-bearing deposit in affiliated bank • prohibits bank from making deposit in affiliated state bank unless state law allows state bank to offer collateral satisfactory under 12 USC 371c • 12 USC 371c prohibits bank from receiving deposits • exempts ordinary course of correspondent business.

7.7400
Deposits by national banks in nonmember banks: restates 12 USC 463 limitation of 10% capital/surplus • recognizes Bank of North Dakota as not being nonmember state bank, permitting member bank deposit to exceed 10%.

7.7405
National banks as depositaries of public money: cites 12 USC 90, 265 • permits bank to request designation as public depository from Treasury Department Bureau of Accounts.

INTERPRETIVE RULINGS (cont.)

12 CFR

7.7410
Pledge of bank assets as security for deposits: prohibits banks from pledging assets to secure private deposits • permits pledging of assets to secure certain public/other deposits.

7.7415
Surety bond in lieu of pledged assets: permits bank to obtain surety bond and pledge assets to reduce premiums if acceptable to public depositor.

7.7485
National banks acting as payroll issuer: permits direct disbursement to customer's employee or credit to employee's account.

7.7515
Service charges on dormant accounts: permits reasonable charges when consistent with deposit contract and approved by board of directors.

7.7517
Accounts without service charge: requires newly organized bank to obtain OCC approval.

7.7519
Loan repurchase agreements: recognizes sale of notes or other paper in loan portfolio under repurchase agreement as borrowing by seller bank • liability equals total obligations subject to repurchase.

INTERPRETIVE RULINGS (cont.)

12 CFR

7.7560
Automatic payment plan account: permits bank to offer savings account that earns dividends • automatically pays accumulated savings/interest in installments to borrower when specified age reached.

BANKING CIRCULARS

BC-121
Remote Disbursement of Customer Checks.

BC-141; Supps. 1-5
Brokered Funds: cautions against "upfront fees"; cautions against brokers requesting fees to fund commissions through "emissions"; cautions against accepting purported OCC credibility statements for large transactions from undisclosed foreign lenders; cautions against involvement in financial transactions without full disclosure; cautions against "prime bank promissory notes" and other questionable instruments.

BC-148
Service charges on dormant Accounts and Abandoned Property Law: (12 CFR 7.7515).

BC-206
Basic Banking Services: low-fee transaction or savings accounts for low- and moderate-income consumers.

BC-224
Federal Recurring Payments Through Financial Institutions by Means Other Than by Check: direct deposit/electronic funds transfer (DD/EFT) payments • Treasury Department imposes interest/penalties for nonposting.

BANKING CIRCULARS (cont.)

BC-241

U.S. Government Check Deadlines: cashing/replacing/initiating claims.

10

FIDUCIARY POWERS OF NATIONAL BANKS

STATUTES

12 USC

92a

Exercise of trust powers by national banks:

permits OCC to grant full range of trust powers by special permit and consistent with authority of competing state banks • requires bank to keep separate books for trust accounts • permits state bank regulators to examine bank trust departments • prohibits checking accounts in trust department • prohibits loans to insiders from trust accounts • permits bank to surrender powers in writing to OCC • permits OCC to revoke authority under certain conditions • requires hearings.

15 USC

77jjj

Acting as indenture trustee:

permits for bank with trust powers • requires minimum capital of $150,000 • rules for holding indenture securities • standards for determining when trustee has conflicting interest and is required to relinquish trusteeship • [stated purpose: to protect public by placing securities under control of trustee or trustees (1 trustee to be U.S. corporation)].

REGULATIONS

12 CFR

Part 5, Subpart B (§§5.22, 5.26)

Organization of a national bank limited to trust powers; Fiduciary powers:

application procedures • forms for trust bank • requires letter of intent for grant of trust powers • OCC considers certain factors • requires OCC approval for bank to exercise trust powers after merger with state bank having trust powers or for conversion of state bank with trust powers into bank.

REGULATIONS (cont.)

12 CFR

Part 9 (except §9.16)

Fiduciary Powers of National Banks and Collective Investment Funds:

cites 12 CFR 5.26 application procedures • OCC considers certain factors • merger conveys trust powers to resulting bank from merging bank if charter number remains same (OCC issues new grant of trust powers if number changes) • requires written policies/procedures for brokerage placement practices • board of directors responsible for administration of trust powers • requires bank to retain legal counsel and bond trust department employees • requires separate books to be kept • requires retention of records for 3 years after termination of account • requires directors to audit trust accounts annually • restricts funds held in trust • prohibits self-dealing • permits bank to charge reasonable fees • requires written plan for collective investment fund to be filed with OCC • rules for administration of collective investment fund and valuation assets • requires annual financial report on fund to customers • requires certain banks to register with OCC as transfer agent • permits bank to appeal to OCC for stay or review of disciplinary actions by clearing agencies.

BANKING CIRCULARS

BC-218

Sweep Fees: trust department short-term cash management programs.

BC-219

12b-1 Funds: subjects mutual fund payment of supplemental fees to 12 CFR 9.12.

BC-233

Acceptance of Financial Benefits by Bank Trust Departments: prohibits discounts, rebates, etc. in exchange for directing trust funds to particular investments • cites 12 CFR §9.12(a).

11

DISSOLUTION/REHABILITATION OF NATIONAL BANKS

STATUTES

12 USC

67 *Compromise of shareholder liability:*	permits receiver of bank to compromise individual liability of any shareholder after OCC/court approval.
91 *Transfers in contemplation of insolvency:*	nullifies all transfers of notes, bonds, deposits or other debts and all transfers of valuables or other assets made to avoid legal requirements applicable to insolvent banks.
181 *Liquidation:*	requires 2/3 shareholder vote • requires 2/3 shareholder vote if purchase/sale agreement with another bank • permits OCC to waive vote in emergency • requires liquidating agent appointed by shareholders to report annually to OCC and shareholders • permits OCC to examine bank.
182 *Notice of liquidation:*	requires board of directors to certify liquidation vote to OCC • requires publication of notice in local newspaper.

12 USC

191 *Appointment of receiver:*	permits OCC to appoint receiver upon finding bank insolvent • requires appointment of receiver under certain conditions • terminates closed receivership fund.
192 *Duties of receiver:*	permits OCC to require bond of receiver • grants receiver full authority to direct affairs of bank • requires receiver to report progress to OCC.
193 *Notice to present claims against receivership:*	requires OCC to publish in local newspaper for 3 months.
194 *Receivership dividends:*	requires OCC to pay ratable dividends on all proved claims • requires excess funds to be distributed to shareholders in proportion to shares held.
196 *Expenses of receivership:*	requires expenses of examination and receivership to be paid out of assets before proceeds distributed • requires protester to pay fees for protesting circulating notes • prohibits bonds deposited to secure notes from being used to pay fees.

12 USC

197

Termination of receivership: after payment of all claims to creditors, requires OCC and FDIC to publish newspaper notice to convene shareholders to decide whether to continue receivership or to elect agent • requires majority vote to decide • requires agent, if elected, to wind up bank affairs and report to U.S. District Court • duties of agent.

197a

Resumption of business: permits OCC to allow bank to resume business if 75% of depositors/unsecured creditors consent in writing to retain deposits at bank.

198

Purchase of property by receiver: permits receiver to petition OCC for right to purchase property in which receiver's trust has interest in order to protect/benefit the trust (i.e. bank assets).

199

Approval of Secretary of the Treasury required: requires Secretary and OCC to approve petition of receiver to purchase property.

200

Authority to draw upon funds deposited with U.S. Treasurer: permits OCC to draw upon funds held in trust for receiver by Treasurer when petition to purchase property is approved.

201

Bank Conservation Act: title.

202

Bank Conservation Act definitions: defines "bank" and "State".

12 USC

203
Appointment of conservator: permits OCC to appoint conservator to take possession and control of bank under certain troubled circumstances • permits judicial review of appointment • permits conservator to request 45-day stay of all actions.

204
Examinations: permits OCC to examine and supervise as long as bank is in conservatorship.

205
Termination of conservatorship: permits OCC to terminate when safe and in public interest • permits OCC to impose and enforce any conditions on resumption of business • permits termination when receiver appointed • requires deposit of net proceeds with court • requires court to distribute equitably.

206
Conservator; powers and duties: confers all powers of shareholders/ directors/officers • subject to OCC rules • permits OCC to require set-aside for depositor withdrawals and creditor payments • OCC fixes compensation.

12 USC

209
Liability Protection:

protects government employees/ agency as conservator according to usual government standards • non-government conservators liable for gross negligence/intentional tortious conduct • permits OCC to indemnify.

210
Bank Conservation Act savings clause:

safeguards OCC powers and powers of other officials.

211
Rules and regulations:

permits OCC to issue rules • requires OCC rules to be consistent with FDIC rules when FDIC is conservator.

212
Bank Conservation Act separability:

reserves right to amend certain statutes.

288
Discontinuance of banking operations by a national bank:

requires cancellation of stock held by insolvent bank in Federal Reserve Bank and use of all cash-paid subscriptions first to pay debts to Federal Reserve Bank • permits OCC to appoint receiver if bank ceases business for 60 days.

12 USC

1821(c),(d)(17)-(19),(m)-(p)

Federal Deposit Insurance Corporation as receiver:

permits OCC to appoint FDIC as conservator • requires OCC to appoint FDIC as receiver whenever OCC invokes receivership statutes • bank in conservatorship remains subject to OCC supervision • confers receivership/ conservatorship powers on FDIC • permits FDIC as conservator/ receiver and conservator appointed by OCC/OTS to disregard transfer, within 5 years before appointment, by institution-affiliated party/debtor if made to hinder/delay/defraud institution/conservator/receiver • permits recovery from transferee, except transferee for value • permits court at request of FDIC as conservator/receiver or conservator appointed by OCC/OTS to issue order placing assets of designated persons under court control • Rule 65 of Federal Rules of Civil Procedure applies, except requirement to show irreparable damage • permits FDIC to organize and OCC to charter new bank in community of closed bank • permits FDIC to and OCC to charter bridge banks to purchase assets/assume liabilities of closed banks for up to 2 years • requires OCC to disclose supervisory records of closed banks to FDIC • prohibits convicted debtor/ substantial borrower in default from purchasing assets from conservator/receiver.

REGULATIONS

12 CFR

Part 5, Subpart D
(§§5.48-5.49)
Voluntary liquidation; Receivership and conservatorship: requires liquidating bank to notify OCC and submit specified reports • forms • prescribes procedures for instituting receiverships • identifies factors for determining insolvency • prescribes claim procedures for non-FDIC receivers.

Part 9
(§9.16)
Receivership or voluntary liquidation of bank: requires receiver to close trust accounts promptly or find substitute fiduciaries • requires liquidating agent to dispose of trust business expeditiously.

BANKING CIRCULARS

BC-247

Application of Securities Laws to Common Trust Funds: registration requirements of 15 USC 77a and 15 USC 80a-1 cover bank common trust funds lacking "*bona fide* fiduciary purpose".

12

INTERNATIONAL BANKING POWERS AND FOREIGN BANK POWERS

STATUTES

12 USC

601
Foreign branches and banking: permits bank with $1,000,000 or more capital/surplus to apply to FRB to open foreign branches and to invest in U.S. or foreign banks principally engaged in foreign banking.

602
Information concerning condition of foreign branches: requires banks to make reports to OCC on demand • requires banks to make reports on investments in foreign banks to FRB on demand • permits FRB to examine foreign branches of banks.

603
Conditions for purchase of stock of foreign banking corporations by national bank: prohibits bank from buying stock until corporation agrees to limit business as FRB prescribes • permits FRB to investigate violations with full subpoena power and order disposal of stock held by bank in violator corporation.

604
Accounts of foreign branches: requires books of each foreign branch to be kept separate from other branches and home office of bank.

12 USC

604a *Regulations pertaining to foreign branches:*	FRB issues rules • permits foreign branch to engage in banking activities customary where branch is located • prohibits merchandising • permits underwriting securities on limited basis as necessary.
618 *National bank investments in banking corporations authorized to do foreign banking business:*	refers to Edge Act Corporations • limits investment to 10% capital/surplus.
1813(l) *International banking facility deposits:*	include obligations payable outside U.S. • refers to FRB Regulation D (12 CFR Part 204).
1813(m)(2) *Foreign bank branch deposits:*	include insured deposits payable in U.S. • FDIC establishes criteria in regulations.
3101-3108 *International Banking Act of 1978:*	permits OCC to allow foreign bank to establish Federal branch/agency in U.S. • OCC issues rules and examines conditions of operation • requires foreign bank to keep certain securities or cash on deposit with member bank • requires foreign bank to select home state • Bank Holding Company Act/FRB rules apply to foreign nonbanking activities • limits interstate branching • requires insurance.

12 USC

3901-3906, 3908-3912

International Lending Supervision Act Of 1983:

requires OCC to evaluate foreign country exposure of banks and establish examination/supervisory procedures • requires OCC to evaluate foreign country ability to repay debt • permits OCC to require banks to keep special reserves for problem loans • accounting for fees in restructured international loans • requires OCC to direct banks to file quarterly reports on foreign country exposure • requires banks to prepare economic feasibility evaluations for foreign loans over $20,000,000 • grants OCC rulemaking authority for banks • applies to bank affiliates • civil money penalties • requires GAO to obtain OCC written approval to audit books • permits GAO to audit OCC international supervisory functions • requires OCC/FRB/FDIC representation at Group of Ten • requires reports to Congress • [stated purpose to encourage prudent private international lending and to enhance coordination among bank regulators].

31 USC

5311-5326

Records and Reports on Monetary Instruments Transactions ("Bank Secrecy Act"):

Treasury Department issues rules • permits Treasury Department to exempt certain transactions • civil money penalties • administrative enforcement procedures • requires banks/certain individuals to maintain records and file reports on monetary instrument/currency transactions involving money entering/leaving U.S. • requires monetary instrument/currency forfeiture plus fine for nonreporting • requires OCC to issue rules and monitor compliance through examination process • requires customer identification to purchase bank checks/cashier's checks/traveler's checks/money orders over $3,000 • permits Treasury Department to require banks to record U.S. coin/currency transactions.

REGULATIONS

12 CFR

Part 5, Subpart B (§§5.23, 5.25)
Establishment of an initial Federal branch (including a limited Federal branch) and a Federal agency of a foreign bank; Application for conversion of a branch or agency operated by a foreign bank or a commercial lending company controlled by a foreign bank into a Federal branch or a Federal agency:

requires application to OCC in Washington, D.C. • requires commencement of business or accomplishment of conversion with 18 months after approval • forms.

Part 5, Subpart C (§5.32)
Additional Federal branch or Federal agency of a foreign bank:

requires application to OCC in Washington, D.C.

Part 5, Subpart D (§§5.41, 5.43)
Relocation of a Federal branch or Federal agency of a foreign bank:

requires application to OCC in Washington, D.C. for change in designation of initial Federal branch/agency to any other Federal branch/agency • approval certificate • forms.

REGULATIONS (cont.)

12 CFR

Part 20

International Operations:

requires bank to give advance notice to OCC of filing of foreign branch application with FRB and within 30 days of branch opening • requires bank to report certain other international activities to OCC within 30 days of event • requires bank to report foreign currency transactions to Treasury Department and OCC • cites 12 USC 3901-3912 • requires banks to establish allocated transfer risk reserves for nonperforming foreign loans cited by OCC • requires amortization of fees for restructured foreign loans over life of loans • rules for accounting for all foreign loan fees • requires quarterly reports to OCC on amount and composition of international assets • requires OCC to disclose on request certain material information on foreign loan concentrations.

REGULATIONS (cont.)

12 CFR

Part 28 (except §28.6)

Federal Branches and Agencies of Foreign Banks:

cites 12 USC 3101-3108 • OCC application process • grants Federal branch/agency same rights/duties as bank • permits FRB to prescribe reserve requirements • requires FDIC insurance for deposits under $100,000 or display of exemption notice • requires separate books • requires on-site service of process • OCC examines.

Interpretive rulings: policy statement on applicability of national banking laws to foreign banks operating at Federal branches and agencies in the U. S.; Community Reinvestment Act is applicable to insured Federal branches.

REGULATIONS (cont.)

31 CFR

Part 103
Financial Recordkeeping and Reporting of Currency and Foreign Transactions: requires certain reports to be filed with Treasury Department • requires filing of certain reports with IRS or Customs • requires filing within 15 days of reportable transaction • requires banks to keep certain records • requires any loan (domestic or foreign) or incoming/outgoing transmission of funds to/from U.S. over $10,000 to be explained and recorded • permits bank to place certain customers on exempt list after obtaining written/signed statement • requires records to be maintained by securities brokers/ dealers, casinos and currency dealers/exchangers • enforcement procedures • civil/criminal penalties • administrative rulings.

INTERPRETIVE RULINGS

12 CFR

7.7012
Foreign operations: permits bank to guarantee obligations of its Edge Act/ agreement corporations and its other instrumentalities abroad.

BANKING CIRCULARS

BC-49; Supp. 5
Financial Recordkeeping and Reporting Regulations: requires filing of currency reports with IRS • retention of copies.

BANKING CIRCULARS (cont.)

BC-124

12 U.S. 72 Citizenship Requirement for Directors: waiver for foreign-owned bank.

BC-193; Supps. 1-5; Supps. 6&7 (Revised); Supp. 8

Financial Recordkeeping and Reporting of Currency and Foreign Transactions Act (Bank Secrecy Act), 31 CFR 103: reporting under 31 CFR 103.23(c) for currency mailed/shipped through postal service, by common carrier or by private courier; change in mailing address for currency transaction reports; delegation of authority to IRS; guidelines for requesting IRS for exemptions from financial reporting requirements; Treasury Department responses to inquiries on the Bank Secrecy Act; procedures for preparation of exemption statements under 31 CFR 103.22; procedure for filing report of International Transportation of Currency or Monetary Instruments (CMIR); reporting of suspicious cash transactions under $10,000.

BC-235

International Payments Systems Risk: credit/sovereign/ operational risks of payments/clearing/settlement systems.

13

CONSUMER/CUSTOMER PROTECTION

STATUTES

12 USC

1735f-5

Sex discrimination prohibited in mortgage lending: prohibits denial of federally related mortgage loan on account of the sex of the prospective borrower • defines "federally related mortgage loan".

2601-2617

Real Estate Settlement Procedures Act of 1974: states purpose to provide consumers with greater and more timely information on nature and costs of settlement • requires use of uniform settlement statement • prohibits kickbacks • rules for escrow accounts • permits recovery of damages for violations in U.S. District Court • permits Secretary of HUD to interpret and grant exemptions [*See* HUD Regulation X: 24 CFR 3500].

12 USC

2801-2809

Home Mortgage Disclosure Act of 1975 (HMDA):

requires banks with offices located in Primary Metropolitan Statistical Areas (PMSAs), MSAs or Consolidated MSAs to compile/disclose number/total dollar amount of home mortgage loans/completed applications made during fiscal year • requires banks to submit data to OCC • FRB issues rules • requires information to be categorized by census tract • OCC enforces for banks • FFIEC compiles/discloses aggregate data [*See* FRB Regulation C: 12 CFR Part 203].

2901-2905

Community Reinvestment Act of 1977 (CRA):

requires OCC to consider in connection with examination each bank's record of meeting community credit needs, including low- and moderate-income neighborhoods • requires record to be weighed in any application for deposit facility (e.g., relocation, merger, branch, etc.) • requires OCC to report annually to Congress • requires OCC to prepare written CRA evaluation at conclusion of bank examination with public section and confidential section.

3806

Adjustable Rate Mortgage (ARM) Caps:

requires creditors to limit maximum interest rate on ARM loans • FRB issues rules • enforcement under Truth-in-Lending Act [*See* FRB Regulation Z: 12 CFR Part 226].

15 USC

1601-1613, 1631-1641

Consumer Credit Cost Disclosure ("Truth-in-Lending Act"): requires creditors to inform prospective borrowers of terms of loan agreements, including finance charge, annual percentage rate (APR), amount financed, etc. • computation of finance charge/ APR • FRB issues rules • OCC enforces for banks • civil/criminal penalties • form of disclosure to borrowers • grants right to rescind loan contract within 3 days if principal dwelling taken as security • requires disclosures for open-end/closed-end credit • requires special disclosures for variable rate mortgage loans • limits/conditions for creditor liability • U.S. District Court jurisdiction • 1 year statute of limitations [*See* FRB Regulation Z: 12 CFR Part 226].

1642-1646

Credit Cards: prohibits issuance of unsolicited cards • limits cardholder liability to $50 for unauthorized use • requires card issuer to notify cardholder of potential liability/means of notification in event of loss • criminal penalties for fraudulent use of cards • permits business cardholders to agree to greater liability for unauthorized use • requires selected banks to submit to FRB semiannual data on credit card price and availability for public dissemination [*See* FRB Regulation Z: 12 CFR Part 226].

15 USC

1647
Home Equity Plans:

covers variable-rate, open-end credit • requires creditor to use interest-rate index publicly available and beyond its control • limits right to terminate • prohibits unilateral change in terms, except in defined circumstances • requires refundability of fees for 3 days after disclosures given [*See* FRB Regulation Z: 12 CFR Part 226].

1661-1665b
Advertising:

rules for advertising credit terms • prohibits certain advertising claims • distinguishes between open-end and closed-end credit • exempts advertising media from liability • prescribes advertisement of fees, initial and periodic interest rates, balloon payments for open-end home equity loans [*See* FRB Regulation Z: 12 CFR Part 226].

1666-1666j
Fair Credit Billing:

rules for consumer resolution of billing errors • requires consumer to notify creditor of error • deadlines for creditor correction • forfeiture of right to collect for failure to comply • rules for length of billing period, crediting of payments, excess payments, return of goods, etc. • prohibits credit card issuer from preventing merchants from offering discounts • court claims/defenses [*See* FRB Regulation Z: 12 CFR Part 226].

15 USC

1667-1667e
Consumer Leasing:

defines "consumer lease" (longer than 4 months and less than $25,000) • requires lessor to give lessee full description of lease terms before consummation • grants lessee rights on residual value of property at expiration of lease • requires certain information to be included in advertising of any lease • civil liability under 15 USC 1640 for violation • 1-year statute of limitations [*See* FRB Regulation M: 12 CFR Part 213].

1671-1677
Garnishment:

limits to 25% of disposable earnings amount of individual's weekly earnings that may be subjected to garnishment • prohibits employer from discharging employee on basis of garnishment • Labor Secretary enforces • permits higher garnishment in certain cases.

15 USC

1681-1681t

Fair Credit Reporting:

defines "consumer reporting agency" • restricts uses of consumer credit reports • requires deletion of obsolete information • requires notification to consumer that certain reports being prepared • permits consumer to see his/her report on request at reasonable time • requires consumer reporting agency to investigate disputed information and correct errors • requires correction to be relayed to persons who used report within previous 2 years • civil liability for violation • 2-year statute of limitations • U.S. District Court jurisdiction • criminal penalties for unauthorized disclosure of reports • OCC enforces for banks.

1691-1691f

Equal Credit Opportunity:

prohibits discrimination by creditor on basis of race, color, religion, national origin, sex, marital status or age • permits certain inquiries • FRB issues rules • FRB may exempt loan class for 5 years • requires special records of business/commercial loans • OCC enforces for banks • actual/punitive damages for violation • U.S. District Court jurisdiction • 2-year statute of limitations [*See* FRB Regulation B: 12 CFR Part 202].

15 USC

1692-1692o

Debt Collection Practices:

prohibits debt collector from identifying self as such when attempting to locate consumer • prohibits debt collector from communicating with consumer at certain times/places • requires debt collector to deal only with attorney if consumer represented by attorney • prohibits harassment/abusive debt collection tactics • prohibits false/misleading means of debt collection • prohibits unfair/unconscionable means of debt collection • requires debt collector to send written notice of facts and right to dispute within 5 days after first communication with consumer • requires debt collector to validate debt if consumer disputes within 30 days of notice • restricts venue of legal actions by debt collectors • prohibits use of deceptive forms • limits civil liability for violation to actual damages plus additional damages not exceeding certain amounts • court considers certain factors • FTC issues rules.

15 USC

1693-1693s

Electronic Fund Transfer (EFT) Act: rules for operation of electronic banking systems/terminals • requires documentation of transfers • requires disclosure of terms/conditions • error resolution procedures • limits consumer liability for unauthorized transfers • liability of bank for damages to consumer • prohibits banks from forcing consumer to use EFT • civil liability for violation • actual/ punitive civil damages for violation • criminal liability for knowing/willful violation • OCC enforces for banks • FRB issues rules [*See* FRB Regulation E: 12 CFR Part 205].

42 USC

3605

Discrimination in residential real estate-related transactions: prohibits bank from denying or structuring home purchase/ construction/improvement/repair/ maintenance loan or financial assistance on basis of race, color, religion, sex or national origin of prospective borrower or associated person or prospective owners/ lessees/tenants/occupants.

4012a, 4104a, 4106, 4128

Flood Disaster Protection Act of 1973: requires OCC to direct banks not to make loans secured by improved real estate located in special flood hazard areas except where covered by flood insurance • requires banks to notify borrowers of flood hazard area designations and availability of federal disaster relief • OCC issues rules.

REGULATIONS

12 CFR

Part 22

Loans in Area Having Special Flood Hazards:

prohibits banks from lending on security of uninsured real estate located in flood zones • exempts self-insured state-owned property • requires bank to give written notice to prospective borrowers of flood hazards and availability of federal disaster relief • requires banks to keep records indicating method used in determining loans subject to this regulation.

Part 25

Community Reinvestment Act (CRA) Regulations:

requires bank annually to delineate its community • requires bank to adopt CRA statement and provide copies to public on request • requires bank to keep public file of CRA comments • requires bank to keep public file of public section of latest CRA Performance Evaluation • requires bank to provide CRA notice in lobby • OCC evaluates CRA performance on basis of factors listed • describes effect of CRA rating on corporate applications.

Interpretive rulings: National banks performing limited services.

REGULATIONS (cont.)

12 CFR

Part 27

Fair Housing Home Loan Data System: requires bank receiving 50 or more home loan applications per year to keep records of home loan activity • permits OCC to require bank to keep log of applications • requires bank to retain records for 25 months • requires OCC to review records during regular examination of bank • permits OCC to require bank to submit data monthly or more frequently • forms.

Part 34 (§§34.8, 34.10)

Adjustable Rate Mortgages (ARMs); Rate changes; Disclosure: requires banks to include maximum interest rate limitation disclosures in consumer credit ARMs required by Truth-in-Lending Act regulations (Federal Reserve Regulation Z: 12 CFR Part 226) [*See* also Series #8, 12 CFR Part 34].

BANKING CIRCULARS

BC-16

Advertisements by National Banks: requires retention of advertising copy to facilitate enforcement of Truth-in-Lending Act and Federal Reserve Regulation Z.

BC-238

Disclosure of CRA-related Corporate Application Decisions: denials and conditional approvals.

14

CRIMES AND PENALTIES

STATUTES

12 USC

1833a

Civil penalties: permits U.S. Attorney General to recover for violations of 18 USC 215, 287, 656, 657, 1001, 1005, 1006, 1007, 1014, 1032, 1341, 1343, 1344 after 8/10/84 • limits penalty to $1,000,000 for single violation and $5,000,000 for continuing violation • prescribes investigatory powers/procedures • requires commencement of action within 10 years.

18 USC

20

Financial institution defined: applies to 18 USC generally.

111

Assaulting, resisting, or impeding certain officers or employees: includes OCC employees • cites 18 USC 1114 • applies when performing official duties • $5,000 fine and/or 3 years in prison • with deadly/ dangerous weapon, $10,000 fine and/or 10 years in prison.

18 USC

212

Loans or gratuities to examiners:

prohibits for officers/directors/employees of insured banks/certain other financial institutions • $5,000 fine and/or 1 year in prison, plus amount of loan/gratuity • applies to government-appointed examiners.

213

Borrowing by examiners:

prohibits government-appointed examiners of insured banks/certain other financial institutions from accepting loan/gratuity from institutions they have authority to examine • $5,000 fine and/or 1 year in prison, plus amount of loan/gratuity, plus removal from office.

215

Bank bribery:

prohibits officers/directors/employees/agents/attorneys of financial institutions/holding companies from corruptly soliciting/receiving anything of value in connection with any institutional business except as provided by law • prohibits anyone from corruptly promising/offering/giving anything of value in connection with institutional business to anyone other than the financial institution or holding company • fine is greater of $1,000,000 or 3 times value of anything given/received and/or 30 years in prison • $1,000 fine and/or 1 year in prison if $100 or less • exempts salary, fees or other compensation paid by financial institution/holding company in usual course of business • requires joint agency guidelines.

18 USC

225

Continuing financial crimes enterprise:

for individual receiving $5,000,000 over 24 months, $10,000,000 fine and/or 10 years in prison • for organization receiving $5,000,000 over 24 months, $20,000,000 fine and/or 10 years in prison • defines as series of violations under 18 USC 215, 656, 657, 1005, 1006, 1007, 1014, 1032, 1341, 1343, 1344 by at least 4 persons in concert.

334

Issuance of Federal Reserve notes:

prohibits unauthorized circulation of Federal Reserve notes or bank notes by agents/employees of FRB or OCC • $5,000 fine and/or 5 years in prison.

335

Circulation of obligations of expired corporations:

applies to corporations created by Act of Congress • prohibits directors/officers/agents from circulating notes, checks, securities, etc. • $10,000 fine and/or 5 years in prison.

641

Public money, property or records:

prohibits theft/conversion/receipt of thing of value of U.S. Government • if over $100, $10,000 fine and/or 10 years in prison • if less than $100, $1,000 fine and/or 1 year in prison.

18 USC

655

Theft by bank examiners:

applies to government-appointed examiners • prohibits theft/concealment of property of value in possession of insured banks/certain other financial institutions • if over $100, $5,000 fine and/or 5 years in prison • if $100 or less, $1,000 fine and/or 1 year in prison • requires removal from office.

656

Theft, embezzlement or misapplication by bank officer or employee:

applies to officers/directors/agents/employees/receivers of insured banks/holding companies/certain other financial institutions/FRB • applies to assets in custody of bank or such individuals • if over $100, $1,000,000 fine and/or 30 years in prison • if $100 or less, $1,000 fine and/or 1 year in prison.

18 USC

709
Use of certain words prohibited:

prohibits "national," "Federal," "United States," "reserve," "Deposit Insurance," "Federal Deposit," "Federal Deposit Insurance," "Federal Deposit Insurance Corporation," "Federal Home Loan Bank," "National Agricultural Credit Corporation," "Federal intermediate credit bank," "Housing and Home Finance Agency," "Federal Housing Administration," "Federal National Housing Association," "Public Housing Administration," "FHA," "Federal Bureau of Investigation," "F.B.I." and "Reconstruction Finance Corporation" • applies to persons engaged in business of banking/ loan/building and loan/brokerage/ factorage/insurance/indemnity/ saving/trust • permits "national" for insurance/indemnity business • prohibits advertisement, publication, etc., where government connection implied • $1,000 fine and/or 1 year in prison.

891
Extortionate credit transactions; definitions and rules of construction:

defines "extended credit," "creditor," "debtor," "repayment of extension of credit," "to collect an extension of credit," "extortionate extension of credit," "extortionate means" and "state" • requires judicial notice of state law.

18 USC

892
Making extortionate extensions of credit:

includes conspiracy • $10,000 fine and/or 20 years in prison • factors constituting *prima facia* evidence of extortion (e.g., annual interest rate above 45%) • permits court to hear evidence of creditor's collection practice reputation in debtor's community.

893
Financing extortionate extensions of credit:

prohibits willful advance of money/ property where reasonable grounds to believe there is extortionate intent • fine is greater of $10,000/ twice value of advance and/or 20 years in prison.

894
Collection of extensions of credit by extortionate means:

$10,000 fine and/or 20 years in prison • permits court to hear evidence of implicit threat and creditor's reputation in relevant community.

896
Effect on State laws:

prohibits preemption by Federal anti-extortionate credit laws of coordinate state laws.

18 USC

955

Financial transaction with foreign governments:

prohibits purchase/sale of obligations of or loan to a government in default of obligations to U.S. • $10,000 fine and/or 5 years in prison • exempts transactions with government that is member of both International Monetary Fund and International Bank for Reconstruction and Development.

981

Civil forfeiture (Money Laundering Control Act of 1986):

permits U.S. Attorney General/ Treasury Dept./USPS to seize property traceable to violation of Bank Secrecy Act (except certain bank currency transactions)/Money Laundering Control Act (except certain bank transactions)/offense against foreign nation involving controlled substances/violation of 18 USC 215, 656, 657, 666, 1001, 1005, 1006, 1007, 1014, 1031, 1032, 1341, 1343, 1344 • customs laws apply • permits transfer of forfeited property to other agencies/states/ foreign nations/victims as restitution • prescribes administrative procedures and venue • prescribes evidentiary rules.

982

Criminal forfeiture (Money Laundering Control Act of 1986):

requires forfeiture to U.S. of property traceable to crime by person convicted of violating Bank Secrecy Act/18 USC 215, 656, 657, 666, 1001, 1005, 1006, 1007, 1014, 1031, 1032, 1341, 1343, 1344, 1956, 1957.

18 USC

1001

Statements or entries generally:

applies to any matter within jurisdiction of U.S. department/agency • prohibits knowing/willful falsification/concealment of material fact or making of fraudulent statement • $10,000 fine and/or 5 years in prison.

1004

Certification of checks:

prohibits before drawer makes covering deposit • prohibits evasion of certification law • applies to officers/directors/agents/employees of insured banks/certain other financial institutions/Federal Reserve Banks • $5,000 fine and/or 5 years in prison.

1005

Unauthorized issuance of obligations or false entries:

applies to officers/directors/agents/employees of insured banks/holding companies/certain other financial institutions • prohibits circulation of bank notes without director authorization or falsification of bank records/reports with intent to injure/defraud/deceive bank/OCC/FDIC/FRB • $1,000,000 fine and/or 30 years in prison.

18 USC

1006

False entries; unauthorized issuance of obligations; receipt of benefits:

prohibits where intent to defraud institution or deceive U.S. Government • applies to officers/agents/employees/persons connected in any capacity with FDIC, NCUA, FHA, FCA, U.S. lending institution, etc. • $1,000,000 fine and/or 30 years in prison.

1013

False representation:

prohibits for obligations of Federal land banks, joint-stock land banks, Federal intermediate credit banks, National Agricultural Credit Corporations • $500 fine and/or 1 year in prison.

1014

Loan and credit applications generally; renewals and discounts; crop insurance:

prohibits knowingly false statements/willful overvaluation of collateral to influence action of bank/federal agency on loan/purchase transaction or acceptance/release/substitution of collateral • $1,000,000 fine and/or 30 years in prison.

1029

Fraud and related activity in connection with access devices:

prohibits knowingly fraudulent use of cards/plates/codes/account numbers/other means of account access • fines/prison terms for first-time/repeat offenders (maximum: $100,000 and/or 30 years) • U.S. Secret Service investigates.

18 USC

1030

Fraud and related activity in connection with computers: prohibits knowingly unauthorized access/use of computer to obtain/tamper with government-restricted information or records of any financial institution • fines/prison terms for first-time/repeat offenders • U.S. Secret Service investigates • exempts lawfully authorized federal/state investigative/protective/intelligence activity.

1032

Concealment of assets from conservator, receiver, or liquidating agent of financial institution: prohibits knowing concealment from/corruptly impeding functions of/corruptly placing beyond reach of FDIC/RTC/conservator appointed by OCC/OTS/NCUA • fine and/or 5 years in prison.

1306

Participation by financial institutions in lotteries: cites 12 USC 25a/similar statutes • $1,000 fine and/or 1 year in prison.

1341

Frauds and swindles: prohibits fraudulent schemes involving counterfeit currency/securities/articles and using the U.S. mails • $1,000 fine and/or 5 years in prison • if violation affects financial institution, $1,000,000 fine and/or 20 years in prison.

1343

Fraud by wire, radio or television: prohibits schemes to defraud of money/property transmitted in interstate/foreign commerce • $1,000 fine and/or 5 years in prison • if violation affects financial institution, $1,000,000 fine and/or 30 years in prison.

18 USC

1344
Bank fraud:

prohibits schemes/artifice to defraud financial institution • $1,000,000 fine and/or 30 years in prison.

1345
Injunctions against fraud:

permits U.S. Attorney General to bring civil suit to enjoin crimes/ potential crimes involving fraud, including bank fraud • permits U.S. Attorney General to bring civil suit to enjoin alienation/disposition of property • permits court to issue restraining order or take other preventative action at any stage of suit.

1510(b)
Obstruction of criminal investigations:

prohibits financial institution officer/director/partner/employee/agent/attorney from divulging existence/contents of subpoena or information furnished to grand jury • fine and/or 5 years in prison for obstructing judicial proceeding • fine and/or 1 year in prison for notification of customer/person named in subpoena.

1517
Obstructing examination of financial institution:

prohibits corrupt obstruction of U.S. agency examination of financial institution • fine and/or 5 years in prison.

18 USC

1906

Disclosure of information by bank examiner:

prohibits to all but officers of examined bank except with written permission of appropriate Federal bank regulator or bank's board of directors or at direction of court or U.S. Congress • $5,000 fine and/or 1 year in prison.

1909

Examiner performing other services:

prohibits for any bank or loan association or its officers/directors/employees if for compensation • $5,000 fine and/or 1 year in prison.

1956

Laundering of monetary instruments (Money Laundering Control Act of 1986):

prohibits financial transactions involving property representing proceeds of unlawful activity with intent to commit crime/conceal source • fine of $500,000/twice value of property and/or 20 years in prison • prohibits transportation of monetary instruments to/from U.S. with intent to commit crime or knowing that instruments represent proceeds of unlawful activity and with intent to conceal source • fine of $500,000/twice value of instruments and/or 20 years in prison • prohibits financial transactions attested by law enforcement officer to involve proceeds of unlawful activity with intent to commit crime/conceal source • fine and/or 20 years in prison • additional civil penalty of greater of value of property/funds/instruments or $10,000 • Justice Department/Treasury Department/USPS investigate.

18 USC

1957

Engaging in monetary transactions in property derived from specified unlawful activity (Money Laundering Control Act of 1986):

prohibits knowing engagement in U.S. or by U.S. person in monetary transaction in criminally derived property valued over $10,000 • fine/twice value of property and/or 10 years in prison • Justice Department/Treasury Department/ USPS investigate.

2113

Bank robbery:

applies to violent crimes committed in banks/credit unions/savings and loan associations/certain other financial institutions • fines/prison terms for taker/knowing receiver of bank property • $10,000 fine and/or 25 years in prison for use of dangerous weapon • requires minimum 10 years in prison and, if jury directs, death for murder or kidnapping while committing robbery or resisting arrest.

3059A

Special rewards for information relating to certain financial institution offenses:

permits U.S. Attorney General to make payments up to $50,000 to persons furnishing unknown information about violations of 18 USC 215, 287, 656, 657, 1001, 1005, 1006, 1007, 1014, 1032, 1341, 1343, 1344 • disqualifies certain government employees/nonoriginal sources of publicly disclosed information/certain institution-affiliated parties/immediate family of violators/co-violators • prohibits court review of U.S. Attorney General's actions • protects "whistleblowers" and permits civil actions to grant relief/attorney fees/ extra recompense to such persons.

18 USC

3293

Financial institution offenses: prohibits prosecution/punishment for violations of 18 USC 215, 656, 657, 1005, 1006, 1007, 1008, 1014, 1341, 1343, 1344 unless indictment/information within 10 years.

Public Law 101-647

[USC cite unassigned as of 12/1/90]

Title XXV, Subtitle H

Financial Institutions Anti-Fraud Enforcement Act of 1990:

Chapter 1 -- Declarations Providing New Claims to the United States (§§2561-2573)

permits any person to file with U.S. Attorney General for violation giving rise to action under 12 USC 1833a • prescribes contents of declaration, including 1 new fact unknown to U.S. Government • requires declarant to maintain confidentiality until U.S. Attorney General responds • disqualifies as declarants certain government employees/co-violators/certain institution-affiliated parties/ immediate family of violators/ nonoriginal sources of publicly disclosed information • if U.S. Attorney General pursues, declarant may select counsel • if criminal conviction, declarant receives award between $5,000 and $100,000 • if U.S. acquires funds/assets, declarant receives percentage • requires U.S. Attorney General to notify declarant of decision not to pursue/judgement/order/ settlement/pendency of investigation or proceeding • if notified that allegations not yet addressed, declarant may request U.S. Attorney General to award contract to pursue case • prohibits court review of U.S. Attorney General's actions, except failure to notify • establishes Financial Institution Information Award Fund • requires U.S. Attorney General to compile semiannual public report • grants declarant 18 USC 3059A protections • U.S. Attorney General issues rules.

Public Law 101-647
[USC cite unassigned as of 12/1/90]

Chapter 2 -- Declarations Providing the United States with New Information Concerning the Recovery of Assets (§§2576-2585)

permits any person to identify assets recoverable by the U.S. to satisfy judgment/settlement for violation of 12 USC 1833a by filing declaration with U.S. Attorney General • prescribes contents of declaration • requires declarant to maintain confidentiality until U.S. Attorney General responds • disqualifies certain government employees/co-violators/certain institution-affiliated parties/ immediate family of violators/ nonoriginal sources of publicly disclosed information • if U.S. Attorney General pursues, declarant may select counsel • if U.S. recovers assets identified by declarant, declarant receives 20%-30% of recovery up to $1,000,000, 10%-20% of recovery up to next $4,000,000, and 5%-10% up to next $5,000,000 • exempts recoveries by OCC and other federal banking agencies • requires U.S. Attorney General to notify declarant of decision not to pursue/judgement/ order/settlement/pendency of investigation or proceeding • if notified that allegations not yet addressed, declarant may request U.S. Attorney General to award contract to pursue case • grants declarants 18 USC 3059A protections • prohibits court review of U.S. Attorney General's actions, except failure to notify • U.S. Attorney General issues rules.

Public Law 101-647

[USC cite unassigned as of 12/1/90]

Chapter 3 -- Rewards for Information Leading to Recoveries, Civil Penalties, or Prosecutions (§§2586-2587)

amends 12 USC 1831k to remove qualifying minimum recovery [*See* Chapter 2 -- General Supervisory Authority of OCC] • adds 18 USC 3059A [*See supra*, this chapter].

Chapter 4 -- Use of Private Legal Resources (§§2588-2594)

permits U.S. Attorney General to retain private legal counsel in civil actions arising from declarations filed under Chapters 1 and 2 of P.L. 101-647 • prescribes terms and conditions of retainer contracts • requires attorney fee contingent on recovery • disqualifies counterclaims not served directly on U.S. Attorney General and U.S. Attorney • permits court to award attorney fees and litigation expenses to U.S. in successful actions • U.S. Attorney General issues rules.

REGULATIONS

12 CFR

PART 21

Minimum Security Devices and Procedures, Reports of Crimes and Suspected Crimes and Bank Secrecy Compliance:

requires bank to file criminal referral forms with OCC to report crimes/ suspected crimes • penalties for failure to file reports.

BANKING CIRCULARS

BC-188; Supp. 1

Bank Bribery Statute: Justice Department guidance for handling prosecutions of federal criminal law (18 USC 215).

BC-222 (Revised)

Bank Bribery Statute: OCC compliance guidelines.

15

MISCELLANEOUS

STATUTES

12 USC

95a
National emergency:

grants President power to investigate/regulate banks and to prohibit/nullify certain transactions in time of war • permits President to freeze foreign assets • permits President to compel recordkeeping/ reports.

95b
Emergency Banking Act:

ratifies closing of banks and other proclamations/actions occurring before/after 3/4/33.

216-216d
Disposition of Unclaimed property from closed national banks:

requires OCC to publish notice in Federal Register by 10/15/83 requiring claims to property to be made within 1 year • requires OCC to determine validity of claims • permits OCC to dispose of unclaimed property after 1 year • permits state/federal court action to determine legal ownership • OCC issues rules.

12 USC

3301-3310

Federal Financial Institutions Examination Council Act of 1978:

creates FFIEC consisting of OCC, FRB, FDIC, OTS, NCUA • requires FFIEC to establish uniform principles/standards/report forms • permits FFIEC to recommend on other supervisory matters • FFIEC trains examiners • liaison with state officials • appraisal subcommittee.

3331-3351

Appraisal Subcommittee of the FFIEC:

prescribes subcommittee structure/ procedures • requires subcommittee to establish uniform standards for real estate appraisals and certification of appraisers • requires subcommittee to monitor state certification agencies • OCC issues rules for banks • defines transactions requiring appraisals • prohibits banks from engaging uncertified appraisers • OCC enforces compliance/imposes penalties for banks.

26 USC

3305(c)

Applicability of State Law to national banks under Federal Unemployment Tax Act:

requires bank to file returns/reports under state law requiring contributions to unemployment fund • requires OCC at request of state to examine banks for correctness of reports.

29 USC

211

Investigations, inspections, records and homework regulations under Fair Labor Standards Act:

(authority of Administrator in Labor Department transferred to EEOC under Reorganization Plan No. 1 of 1978) permits EEOC to gather data on wages/hours/other employment conditions in banks • permits EEOC to enlist investigative services of state agencies • requires banks to keep certain records and report to EEOC as EEOC requires.

INDEX

D

E

F

G

K–L

S

T

U